W9-CNJ-800

COLOSSAL
CANADIAN
FAILURES

COLOSSAL CANADIAN FAILURES

A Short History of Things That Seemed Like a Good Idea at the Time

Randy Richmond and Tom Villemaire

THE DUNDURN GROUP
TORONTO

Copyright © Randy Richmond and Tom Villemaire, 2006

All rights reserved. No part of this publication may be reproduced, stored in a retrieval system, or transmitted in any form or by any means, electronic, mechanical, photocopying, recording, or otherwise (except for brief passages for purposes of review) without the prior permission of Dundurn Press. Permission to photocopy should be requested from Access Copyright.

Copy-editor: Jennifer Gallant
Design: Jennifer Scott
Printer: University of Toronto Press

Library and Archives Canada Cataloguing in Publication

Richmond, Randy, 1958-
Colossal Canadian failures 2 : a short history of things that seemed like a good idea at the time / Randy Richmond and Tom Villemaire.

Includes bibliographical references.
ISBN-10: 1-55002-618-6
ISBN-13: 978-1-55002-618-4

1. Canada--History--Miscellanea. 2. Failure (Psychology). I. Villemaire, Tom II. Title.

FC25.R55 2006   971   C2006-901337-3

1   2   3   4   5   10   09   08   07   06

We acknowledge the support of the **Canada Council for the Arts** and the **Ontario Arts Council** for our publishing program. We also acknowledge the financial support of the **Government of Canada** through the **Book Publishing Industry Development Program** and **The Association for the Export of Canadian Books**, and the **Government of Ontario** through the **Ontario Book Publishers Tax Credit program**, and the **Ontario Media Development Corporation**.

Care has been taken to trace the ownership of copyright material used in this book. The author and the publisher welcome any information enabling them to rectify any references or credits in subsequent editions.

J. Kirk Howard, President

Printed and bound in Canada.
Printed on recycled paper.

www.dundurn.com

Dundurn Press
3 Church Street, Suite 500
Toronto, Ontario, Canada
M5E 1M2

Gazelle Book Services Limited
White Cross Mills
High Town, Lancaster, England
LA1 4XS

Dundurn Press
2250 Military Road
Tonawanda, NY
U.S.A. 14150

TABLE OF CONTENTS

ACKNOWLEDGEMENTS

This book would not have been possible without the encouragement of some and the discouragement of others. We responded equally well to those who considered our first book on failure a sign of success and those who considered it a sign of insanity.

Somewhere in the middle, as he should be, is Dundurn's editorial guru, Barry Jowett, who after considerable thought decided we could do a second book based on the sales of the first. Of the original, Jowett said, "It didn't tank." We have made that the official slogan of our work.

Others at Dundurn include boss Kirk Howard, sales guru Beth Bruder, copy editor Jennifer Gallant, and designer Jennifer Scott.

Our thanks also go to our employers, Osprey Media and the *London Free Press*, for time given to work on the book.

Thanks to more of the tipsters who keep us in business: Chip Martin, Ken Whiteman, Patrick Maloney, John Herbert, Joe Martin, and Jamie Hunter. We didn't use all of your tips. In fact, some kept us busy on wild goose chases, but we appreciated the support.

Thanks too to historians everywhere, especially those who toil on so-called local histories. Without them breaking the path, we would have remained forever in the woods.

And thanks to our families. Sandra Richmond (Tom's wife, Randy's sister) gave us amazing editorial help and legal advice. It helps to have a former editor and current entertainment lawyer in the family. Janice

Richmond (Randy's wife, Tom's sister-in-law — it gets confusing) uncomplainingly took on all the unglamorous day-to-day chores so we could write this book and, along with Rebecca, Sawyer, and Molly, gave us unwavering moral support. Read the books, kids. There will be a test.

And finally, thanks to all those Canadians who never let an idea pass them by, however bad, and to Canadians who let their fellow citizens with great ideas fall into the cracks. There would be no book without them.

INTRODUCTION

Without failure, there would be no Canada.

Without bungles, boondoggles, mishaps, and mistakes of various degrees, we'd be American or part of France or obedient to a noble class based in England instead of the class clowns based in Ottawa. We'd have cities in different places than they are now. We'd have farms in the hinterland and hinterland where there are now farms. We'd have a happy Quebec. Maybe.

We'd have an unhealthy respect for politicians and government.

We'd think the other guy was better than us. That would pretty well ruin our democratic principles.

We'd have fewer elections.

We'd have fewer laughs.

We wouldn't have a second *Colossal Canadian Failures*.

Just as in our first book (available at garage sales, sidewalk sales, and on those bargain tables outside your local bookstore), we present a smattering of failures here. We label them *colossal* because of the difference between the intent and the result, and because *colossal* and *Canadian* sound good together.

Some of them changed the history of the entire country. Some changed the history of a province or a town, and some just made us giggle or shake our heads in wonder.

All of them made us realize that what failure after failure has made Canada is the true north, strong and free — free to make mistakes, that is.

CHAPTER I
POLITICS

Canadian politicians bring a certain *je ne sais quoi* to life, besides butchered French. Whether they're trying to put down rebellions among the populace or trying any desperate measure to get elected, they have a style that makes an ordinary Canadian proud to be an ordinary Canadian, and not a politician.

I'll be a unifying force. Everyone will hate me.

When revolution was brewing in Upper Canada — that would be Ontario nowadays — the British government realized a strong, smart leader was needed.

So whom did they send to settle the problem? Francis Bond Head, a man that England's *Punch* eventually referred to as "Sir Francis Wronghead." So much for the strong, smart leader.

Bond Head had served in the Royal Engineers, so he knew how to blow things up. He had applied for but was turned down as the head of the London police when he returned from military service, which included serving at Waterloo. He had written a number of excellent travel articles. He had demonstrated the military usefulness of the lasso. For this he was knighted.

But — no background in politics.

He was as shocked as anyone when a rider arrived at his home in the middle of the night to rouse him from his warm bed with the news.

Sir Francis Bond Head was a good solider and engineer but a lousy politician.

His own father had run from the United Kingdom after spending the family's wealth on gambling and the high life. His father had kept in touch with him, asking for money on a regular basis. The possibility of elevating his family seemed near with the offer from the Crown to run Upper Canada. He asked for a baronetcy and got it. And off he went to the New World.

A letter to his own son, Frank, revealed Bond Head's bewilderment at the posting: "You will think it rather a strange event when I tell you that I have come in to take leave of the King on assuming the Government of Canada. I know very little more than yourself [about the running of a country]."

But that didn't stop him from trying. When he and his family arrived in York, they were greeted with banners calling Bond Head a reformer. In fact, Bond Head wasn't a reformer. He was a conservative and he snuggled right in with the Family Compact — the elite group of well-to-do families and wealthy merchants who controlled the government because they had the right to overrule the elected assembly, which represented the vast majority of not-so-wealthy people who weren't in the Family Compact.

The Family Compact thought the common folk were a bit revolting. Soon they would find them more so.

In fact, it was unhappiness with the Family Compact that was causing the rebellion. Bond Head had been in town for only a week when he started to annoy the vast majority of the population. He had diagnosed the problem and was ready to proffer a prescription. As a "political physician" he lacked nothing but an understanding of the situation. When it came to the reformers, he said he would "mercilessly destroy them root and branch" and would "very soon be able to report proudly that the grievances of Upper Canada were defunct because I had veni-ed, vidi-ed, vici-ed them."

As you might imagine, this did not end the talk of revolution.

William Lyon Mackenzie had garnered a reputation in Great Britain and was warmly greeted by the politician in charge of the United Kingdom's colonies. Mackenzie's book of complaints against the Family Compact was taken seriously in Great Britain and Bond Head was told to address the concerns. He responded by calling the document "Mr. Mac's heavy book of lamentations."

To settle things once and for all, Bond Head dissolved the government and called an election. And he ran a good old-fashioned election. By Upper Canadian standards, that meant corruption, violence, intimidation, riots, and a careful consideration of where the polling stations were positioned.

Orangemen — members and supporters of the Family Compact — played a prominent role. "Orangemen running up and down the streets crying five pounds for a liberal [reformer] and if any man said a word contrary to their opinion he was knocked down; and all this in the presence of magistrates, and judges, who made use of no means to prevent these outrages. The election occurred on the first of July, 1836, and it was a gathering which for riot and drunkenness exceeded everything I had ever seen before," wrote W.H. Merritt.

After the election, flushed with his inevitable victory, Bond Head wrote to the British Colonial Office, "Nothing can be brighter than the moral and political state of the Canadas. All is sunshine and colour of rose."

Shortly after this arrived in Britain, rebellion broke out in Lower Canada, now Quebec, and Upper Canada, now Ontario.

When the rebellion broke out in Upper Canada, Bond Head and his friends joined the rank of the militia as they marched north on Yonge Street. With a band marching along, playing "Heart of Oak," they trooped up to Gallows Hill, and it is not far from there that they ran headlong into the rebels marching south. In the militia ranks were trained soldiers, many who had fought with Lord Wellington in France and Spain, including Bond Head. In the far larger body of the rebels were farmers and store clerks but not many soldiers.

Volleys were fired from both sides before both sides retreated. The militia were convinced the overwhelming numbers of the rebels would swarm them and the rebels were convinced the crack shots of the former British soldiers (whom they still held in high regard) would cut them to pieces.

Bond Head left Upper Canada in the spring of 1838, convinced he had saved the country.

And he had in a way. His inept handling had brought the boil of the Family Compact to a head, so to speak, and allowed it to be lanced. Not that he was thanked for his efforts. Bond Head snuck out of the country, crossing the ice from Kingston to the United States in fear for his life.

In 1867, Head requested and received an appointment to the Queen's Privy Council for his "contribution to the development of Canada." He died at his home in Croydon at the age of eighty-two on July 20, 1875, still convinced he had saved a country.

Oh for crying out loud, flip a coin

How hard can it be to count votes?

Other than in Florida.

Or in North York, Ontario.

In the November 1988 federal election, Progressive Conservative candidate Michael O'Brien was declared the winner over Liberal Maurizio Bevilacqua by fifty-eight votes. The Tories had the seat.

O'Brien had barely had time to celebrate when, a few days later, an automatic recount by Elections Canada gave the election to Bevilacqua by six votes.

A judicial recount after that reversed the first reversal and gave O'Brien the seat by ninety-nine votes. O'Brien trundled off to Ottawa.

He lasted all of fifty-five days before a second judicial recount by the Ontario Supreme Court changed everything again. Bevilacqua was declared the winner, by seventy-seven votes.

Now it was his turn to trundle off to Ottawa. One hopes neither one got any money to redecorate their offices.

O'Brien appealed the Ontario Supreme Court count. Elections Canada was accused of rejecting dozens of voters who were eligible to vote and accepting dozens of voters who were not eligible to vote.

The judge threw out the entire election.

Somehow North York managed to stumble along, MP-less, until a December 1990 by-election. By then the fortunes of the Tories in Ontario were sliding. The NDP had even won the provincial election that fall. Perhaps the good people of North York were also tired of the entire mess. They voted in Bevilacqua by seven thousand votes.

No kittens or reptiles were harmed in the production of this story

What do you get when you put together campaign workers, a dumb joke, and a press release?

An election nightmare.

In the midst of the fall 2003 Ontario election campaign, Conservative party workers sent out an email that accused Liberal Leader Dalton McGuinty of being, of all things, "a kitten eater."

"Dalton McGuinty: He's an evil reptilian kitten-eater from another planet," said the release straight from Conservative Premier Ernie Eves's campaign headquarters.

McGuinty had a reputation for being wooden, dull, and maybe a little reptilian. And everyone knows that all politicians are from another planet. As for evil, how could anyone tell? He hadn't actually been elected yet.

But no one had ever seen him eat a kitten.

Jokes that sound fun in college dorms and campaign offices aren't as funny in the real world. The media jumped all over the moronic message.

Eves tried to downplay the comment. "I think somebody had either way too much coffee this morning or had way too much time," he told reporters the morning the release came out.

McGuinty had some fun with the release: "I have eaten calf, I'll admit to that."

The press release grew in notoriety. The Conservative government was embroiled in a tainted meat scandal that year. So a Liberal strategist had no problem in pointing out that at least the kitten meat had cleared inspection.

The press release probably didn't cost the Conservatives the election, but it certainly didn't help their cause. For some, it symbolized the sarcastic and hard edge the Conservatives had brought to Ontario politics for the past decade. For some, it symbolized the mudslinging the Conservatives seemed to enjoy a little too much. For others, it symbolized party stupidity.

The Conservatives lost the election. Eves resigned as party leader. McGuinty became premier.

And rancid tuna spreads better

Cabinet ministers come and cabinet ministers go, but surely Brian Mulroney's Conservative government deserves some kind of recognition for the sheer number and consistency of ministers forced to resign. From 1984 to 1993, Mulroney averaged one cabinet minister forced to resign each year under a cloud.

Here's the tally:

1985
- Defence Minister Robert Coates, after visiting a strip club in West Germany while on official business.
- Fisheries Minister John Fraser, after approving 1 million tins of rancid tuna as fit for public consumption.
- Communications Minister Marcel Masse, over allegations of violations to the Canada Elections Act. He was later cleared.

1986
- Regional Industrial Expansion Minister Sinclair Stevens, because of conflict of interest allegations in a $2.6-million loan to a family company.

1987
- Minister of State for Transport Andre Bissonnette, after the RCMP investigated him for land speculation.
- Minister of Public Works Roch Lasalle, after being charged with demanding a bribe and taking money from a business looking for a few favours. The charges were later dropped.

1988
- Supply and Services Minister Michel Cote, over conflict of interest allegations involving a loan.

1989

- Consumer and Corporate Affairs Minister Bernard Valcourt, after pleading guilty to impaired driving.

1990

- Fitness and Amateur Sport Minister Jean Charest, after trying to talk to a judge about a case.

1991

- Housing Minister Alan Redway, after joking about having a gun while getting on a plane in Ottawa.

Fisheries boss John Fraser's tuna scandal deserves special attention.

In the spring of 1985, Fisheries inspectors deemed about 1 million tins of New Brunswick tuna unfit for human consumption. The tuna, federal inspectors said, was rancid and decomposing. Star-Kist Canada Inc., which ran the St. Andrews, New Brunswick, tuna plant, didn't like that ruling. Neither did New Brunswick Premier Richard Hatfield. So they called up federal Fisheries Minister John Fraser. The plant employed four hundred people, they pointed out. Something like this could shut it down. No worries, Fraser said. He ordered the tuna released for sale on April 29.

Five months later, on September 17, CBC's *Fifth Estate* exposed what became known as Tunagate. For a few days, Fraser and Mulroney tried to avoid the mighty big net of public opinion coming their way. Fraser hung on as long as he could. First, he claimed sending the tuna off was merely a judgement call.

"There was never a question of health," he told the House of Commons. "What there is is a question of esthetics." He later told reporters, "Almost all fish will have some scientifically proven taint or some scientifically proven decomposition."

Only twenty-four hours later, Fraser flipped and asked the federal government to confiscate the 1 million tins of rancid tuna. Many grocery stores, more adept than cabinet ministers at gauging public opinion, had already dumped their stocks.

The tuna scandal threatened to taint Mulroney himself, as it turned out that eight Conservative MPs had discussed the rancid tuna a week before it was released for public consumption. The MPs said they never told their boss, Mulroney, about the meeting.

"That is hard to swallow," said Liberal Leader John Turner.

Six days after the scandal broke, Fraser resigned. Because of the bad publicity, the tuna plant Fraser and Premier Hatfield were trying to protect was shut down, and four hundred people were thrown out of work.

CHAPTER 2
SHIPS

From sea to shining sea, from Great Lakes to little rivers, Canada is noted for its waterways. Most of the time, we've managed to navigate them quite well. Most of the time.

Maybe the Canadians put in a bad propeller on purpose

An American man *almost* became a pirate on Georgian Bay with Canada's help. To be an effective pirate, you usually need to be a stealthy sort. Oh, and a good ship comes in handy too. Neither of those really applied to Jacob Thompson.

Born May 15, 1810, in Leasburg, Caswell County, North Carolina, he was a studious and bright child. After being the valedictorian of his class at the University of North Carolina in 1831, he was appointed a tutor at the university. He resigned to study law and later became licensed to practise in the courts of North Carolina. His brother convinced him to move to Mississippi, and he joined the Confederate Army at the beginning of the American Civil War.

In 1863, he returned home to Mississippi to run for office in the state legislature. After being re-elected, he was asked by the president of the Confederacy to go back to work for the army as a fifth columnist.

A fifth column is a group of people who secretly support or sympathize with a country's enemies and engage in clandestine sabotage and espionage for that enemy inside the country. Fifth columnists were the source of a great many wild plans.

Jacob Thompson's plan was simple and daring — he and his crew would take a ship into the upper Great Lakes and capture and plunder or destroy American ships by ramming them, and then quickly retreat into the shallow island- and rock-filled waters of Georgian Bay, where they could hide. Thompson himself would lead the expedition of piracy.

Thompson had many friends in Canada, where there was a large num-

The Free Press: Osprey Media.

Jacob Thompson planned to be a pirate on an expedition of terror on the Great Lakes during the American Civil War, but the propeller on his boat kept falling off.

ber of people who sympathized with the southern rebels. Great Britain sided with the rebels in an unofficial manner, as a matter of expediency. While John Graves Simcoe, the British lieutenant-governor of Upper Canada, had outlawed slavery in Upper Canada in the 1700s, Great Britain itself was not so choosy about who worked the cotton fields of the southern states. It needed cotton for the huge British textile industry. With such support in the mother country, the sympathy in Upper Canada was predictable. And in fact Thompson had run a number of raids into the northern states from Canada before setting up shop in Toronto.

So it wasn't difficult for Thompson to buy a boat in Toronto from Dr. James Bates, originally of Louisville, Kentucky. The steamer, called the *Georgian*, was delivered to the Confederate fifth column at Port Colborne, Upper Canada, on November 1, 1864. The price was about $16,000, paid to A.M. Smith & Co.

The *Georgian*, a product of the Port McNicoll shipyards, was described by U.S. Vice Consul General Thurston Montreal as "a new vessel, built some year and a half since on the Georgian Bay, by [George] H. Wyatt and others, and has, I believe, made one trip across the Atlantic. She is a splendid vessel, built with great care, a fast sailer, and would be capable of doing immense injury to the shipping on the Lakes." He noted the Confederate agents "claim that she is particularly adapted to the lumber trade, as she carries heavy loads with light draft and intend to strengthen her beams for towing."

As it turned out, he may have been exaggerating a bit. By the time the Confederates got the ship, the smokestack had been cut down, giving it a "rakish appearance, like that of a fast raider." Apparently, the modification was done for looks only and had no real effect on the ship's speed. And, once purchased, the boat was further modified with a bow reinforced for ramming commercial ships — not something that lends itself to fast escapes. So the ship, which was plagued with mechanical problems throughout its pirating career, may not have been quite so "splendid" as advertised.

As for Thompson, he already had quite a reputation as a rebel sympathizer on both sides of the border. He barely concealed his Confederate Army profession and actually used the lobby of a Toronto hotel to run his operations. So when he bought the boat, everyone knew it. And when the boat left for Lake Erie from Lake Ontario, everyone knew it.

It's not clear why Thompson would have told the captain to make for Buffalo, but he did. While there, he barely escaped capture when the mayor of Buffalo recognized him and the ship. The mayor called for help and the Union government sent out the USS *Michigan*. The government also equipped two tugboats with guns to protect the city and the east end of Lake Erie. The *Georgian* slipped out of the Buffalo dock but was boarded by the crew of the *Michigan* when they caught up with her in Lake Erie.

No contraband was found and no Confederate soldiers were aboard, so the boat was allowed to continue on its way, with the *Michigan* following close behind. Making no attempt to escape, the *Georgian* poked along — mostly because by this point it had developed a wobbly propeller.

In December, the *Georgian* stopped at Port Stanley to repair the loose propeller. And then again at Sarnia when the propeller became loose again. The *Georgian* made its way past Detroit, causing quite a stir. The *Georgian* was seized again. Again, nothing was found to justify holding the boat and it was allowed to continue.

The *Georgian* ran into more trouble in Lake Huron. The propeller was still not functioning properly, so a new one was ordered and shipped to Collingwood for installation. Before the ship could make it there, she was boarded near Port Elgin. Again, no contraband, weapons, or Confederate spies were found. She put in to Collingwood for the propeller repair and was searched again.

Canadian authorities were going to condemn the boat as a navigational hazard because of the wonky propeller, but the ship's captain promised it would be good as new with the new propeller and the boat was allowed to leave. The captain said the *Georgian* was going to get into the lumber trade, moving logs from Georgian Bay to Saginaw Bay. Before the end of the shipping season, she made a run for Bruce Mines and then returned to winter in Collingwood.

By the start of the shipping season of 1865, the Civil War was almost over. But Canadian authorities noted the *Georgian* was being outfitted with a new mast. On April 7, 1865, a raid on the boat turned up a letter

Don't sail it into action, it might get some action

The War of 1812 was an odd thing.

There were moments of brilliance on both sides and a lot more moments of stupidity.

One of the decisions of questionable judgement was the construction of the *St. Lawrence*, a 112-gun ship of the line — the equivalent of a battleship today — on Lake Ontario.

It was bigger than the ship Lord Nelson had when he defeated the French forces at Trafalgar nine years earlier.

It was a monster of a ship, 1,200 tonnes and crewed by one thousand men. Immense resources were used to build the ship. Two hundred shipwrights and hundreds of other skilled and unskilled hands fell to work on the thing at Kingston, Ontario. The wood and guns involved could have built two or three frigates.

After it was built, it was hard to find enough skilled sailors, so crew had to be taken from other ships, making those ships less effective in battle.

It cruised Lake Ontario, but the British were too shy to use it, fearing that the loss of this single monument would be too large a blow to morale and money.

That rendered it an expensive decoration.

After the war, there wasn't much for the *St. Lawrence* to do and it was too big to go down the St. Lawrence River, so it was sunk off Kingston Harbour, where today it's a popular dive site.

dated October 1864 to the captain of the *Georgian* to modify the boat so it could "employ greek fire" — burning material hurled by catapult onto a target, like, oh, say, another boat. And there was another letter instructing the *Georgian* captain to procure the "finest waterproof caps for the troops." Given that the boat was supposed to be a commercial logging craft — with no "troops" on board — the Canadian government seized the ship.

Thompson's pirating days might have been over, but the *Georgian's* sailing days weren't. After the war, the 130-foot, 377-ton passenger freighter was sold to G.T. Denison of Ontario and embarked on a career of twenty years of legitimate business. On May 9, 1888, the *Georgian* became stranded off Cape Rich (now a part of the old Meaford Tank Range, northwest of Meaford) and was sunk by ice. It now rests on the bottom of the bay in about one hundred metres of water.

Always listen to the captain

The captain complained before setting sail that the two-masted, eighty-foot vessel was unseaworthy. Storms were brewing on Lake Ontario. The ship was full to the rails of important people.

No matter. The HMS *Speedy* had to sail, government officials said. It had to make it to a new town called Newcastle, because justice had to be served, the navy had to be put in its place, the town had to showcase its new courthouse in order to become an important district capital, and the natives had to be taught a lesson.

The schooner ran aground even before it left the harbour at York. It should have been a sign. Two hours later, though, on that afternoon of October 7, 1804, the *Speedy* pulled itself off the shoal and carried on.

It carried a who's who of Upper Canada's justice system — the solicitor general, a judge, two lawyers, a law student, defence witnesses, and the accused — all heading for a trial that began with a killing a year earlier.

Details of that killing are vague and contradictory. A white man with the last name Cozens killed a native named Whistling Duck in about 1803. Some historians believe the killer was Samuel Cozens, a troubled soul who drifted from job to job, but a troubled soul with connections to important people in Upper Canada. Cozens was not arrested. There was no trial. A year later, angry that no one had brought Cozens to justice, another native and perhaps a relative or friend of Whistling Duck named Ogetonicut killed a white trader named John Sharpe. Ogetonicut was arrested. And this time, there was to be a trial.

Much depended on this trial. The killing took place in the Newcastle District. That meant the town of Newcastle would host the trial. The town was only two years old but already boasted a courthouse and jail and one-acre lots for the first families. Plans were in the works for a hospital and school. Newcastle, it was hoped, would become the capital of the district. Perhaps someday it would become as important as York, the muddy capital to the west on Lake Ontario.

The so-called roads from York to Newcastle were barely passable, so it was decided to ship the whole court to Newcastle. That was a mistake. The Lake Ontario Navy wasn't up to standards of the British Royal Navy. Poor pay and poor working conditions made it hard to find enough crew for ships, never mind men who knew what they were doing.

In Britain, naval officers were under command of the Admiralty, a powerful office. In Upper Canada, the boats and captains were under command of the land-based military establishment. The long-established rivalry between sailors and soldiers in the British Empire wasn't based solely on different clothing. The navy wasn't that good at understanding what soldiers did, and military command on land was often equally bad at understanding how ships should be operated.

Ships in Upper Canada were often built in a hurry, with unseasoned lumber, and often rotted out within a few years. There simply weren't enough skilled craftsmen to build the ships properly. Built in 1798 under those exact conditions, the *Speedy* wasn't under sail for more than a year before it needed repairs for leaks, probably because of dry rot in the fresh timber.

By 1804, the *Speedy* was nearing the end of its natural life on the lakes. When it was ordered to head to Newcastle, its captain, Thomas Paxton, told Lieutenant-Governor Peter Hunter the ship was not seaworthy. Hunter, a landsman, did not care what the captain thought. So the *Speedy* went into the storms that October 7, got grounded, got off the shoal, and continued on.

A few hours out of York it reached present-day Oshawa, where two key witnesses to the killing, the Farewell brothers, were to be picked up. The Farewell brothers, perhaps eyeing the waterlogged, overloaded vessel, declined to board. We'll keep going in our canoe, they said. We'll meet you there.

The *Speedy* reached the harbour at Newcastle, one hundred miles away, in twenty-four hours, on the evening of October 8. The vessel was only an hour from safety when a fierce storm blew up and drove *Speedy* away from the harbour. Waterlogged, the waves breaking over deck and the bilge pumps working as fast as they could, the *Speedy* began to founder. Those on shore lit a bonfire for a beacon.

There are no accounts of what happened aboard the *Speedy*. The outcome became clear a few weeks later when debris from the wreck began to wash ashore. All aboard drowned, including the prisoner, bound in chains in the hold.

The sinking of the *Speedy* shook Upper Canada. The legal community lost many prominent and promising members. "[N]or does it often happen that such a number of persons of respectability are collected in the same vessel," wrote the *Gazette* in a November 3, 1804, article about the disaster.

"It is somewhat remarkable," the *Gazette* continued, " that this is the third or fourth accident of a similar nature within these few years, the cause of which appears worthy [of] the attention and investigation of persons conversant in the art of ship-building."

No investigation was made.

The sinking also ended the grand plans for Newcastle. In February 1805, a petition signed by 135 people in York asked the House of Assembly to abandon plans for a district capital in the "inconvenient" location of Newcastle. The honour went instead to Amherst, which was twenty-four miles closer to York and is now called Cobourg. The original Newcastle disappeared, although the present-day one was built later on to the west. Where the grand district capital was to be built sits Presqu'ile Provincial Park and some cottages.

If you're going to push the limits, you'd better make sure they fit

Captain Augustus A. Pickering built and sailed ships and was pretty good at it. His greatest success was building and sailing the first commercial ship to Chicago. The *Illinois* was eighty feet long, schooner rigged with two masts, and rated at eighty-one tonnes.

On May 12, 1834, the *Illinois* boarded passengers in Sackets Harbour with farm equipment and other cargo and set off for Chicago. No other ship of the size of the *Illinois* had attempted this voyage before.

With 104 passengers, the ship made the trip in a little over a month only to find the river mouth blocked with a sandbar about four feet below the surface. But the people of Chicago were so excited at the prospect of commercial shipping finally arriving at their town that they hauled Pickering's boat over the sandbar with sheer brute force.

Pickering was highly regarded as a Great Lakes captain for bringing such a large vessel through the canal and into the Midwest. His design and construction of the *Illinois* was good enough that when the vessel's final days came — twenty-six years later in July 1865 in a storm off Vermillion, Ohio — it was the oldest on the Great Lakes.

As a shipbuilder, Pickering wanted to build ships that just fit in the canal — thereby capitalizing on every possible inch of space. He was so elated over his success with *Illinois* that he kept pushing the limits.

The *Niagara* was built in the same Sackets Harbour yard that produced the *Illinois*. But the *Niagara* was much bigger. And it held a lot more passengers. And a lot more freight.

And so off it went across Lake Ontario to the Welland Canal and … bump.

The *Niagara* was an inch too wide to make it through the locks.

Augustus and his brother-in-law, Winslow, backed the ship up and studied it. Both were convinced they could shave an inch off the sides. Eventually it was narrowed enough to fit the locks.

Unfortunately, Augustus didn't live to see it. He was so upset over the mistake that he went without sleep trying to figure out how to correct it. Eventually, exhausted and despondent, he took his own life.

Can't we just let them rest in peace?

On August 20, 1852, the *Atlantic*, a steamer packed with passengers, collided with the *Ogdensburg* on Lake Erie. The *Atlantic* was uninsured and her valuable cargo sank in 165 feet of water, seven miles inside the Canadian border. Between 150 and 250 passengers died in the tragedy.

Almost immediately there were attempts to salvage the wreck and retrieve the cargo. And, almost as quickly, there were lawsuits. A series of failed salvage attempts would take place over the next 150 years, driven by the approximately $35,000 (in 1852 dollars) of American Express gold contained in the *Atlantic*'s safe.

In October 1852, a diver named Johnny Green spent time and money developing special air pumps to allow him to reach the bottom — an unreachable depth until this point. The old depth record was 126 feet, but Green set a new depth record of 154 feet, down to the wreck of the *Atlantic*. Green didn't get the safe. He managed to cut it loose, but on returning to the surface to bring cables down to lift the safe to the surface, Johnny Green almost died of the bends.

In 1853 a man named Lodner Phillips felt he had the answer. Give the man a cigar. Actually, that was the name of his answer. The *Marine Cigar*. Not exactly a glamorous name. But it accurately described the look of the forty-foot-long tube that was fourteen feet in diameter. And, yes, it was a submarine. Built by Phillips in Michigan City, Indiana, in 1851, it was nicknamed "Fool Killer."

The *Marine Cigar* was brought to the lake by train and then transported out on a tender. In the first dive, the crew detected leakage occurring at one hundred feet, and it was taken to the surface for repairs. It was sent down in an unmanned test dive, but it became fouled in the *Atlantic*'s masts and sank. If the crew had hurried to attempt salvage, it would have taken them with it.

Elliott Harrington, of a rival salvage company, recovered the treasure June 27, 1856. A court battle ensued and most of the money was returned to its original owners, with only $7,000 going to Harrington and his backers.

The *Atlantic* was a fairly new ship when it sank. It was reputed to have gilded interiors, tapestries, and rosewood furnishings. This caused the continuation of a number of attempts at salvage that involved diving bells and other stunts, all doomed to failure.

Finally, the *Atlantic* was forgotten. Until the 1980s.

Mike Fletcher, a local Canadian diver from Port Dover, rediscovered the wreck. He retrieved some items, including the ship's bell, and gave this salvage to the government agency in charge of historic wrecks. Fletcher marked the site and anticipated that it would become a part of Ontario's heritage and a historic site now that he had brought the *Atlantic* back into the minds of the public.

Unfortunately, it also came into the minds of an American diving company out of San Pedro California, the Mar Dive Group. They had different plans for the wreck. Using Fletcher's buoy to explore the site, they took a pile of booty from the wreck to California and, according to the firm Beard, Winter, Barristers and Solicitors, hired by Fletcher, "obtained a default/consent and unopposed judgment in the United States District Court, Central District of California, giving it ownership, salvage, etc. rights to the *Atlantic*. The California court issued an order permitting them to arrest the *Atlantic*."

At an Ontario court hearing, Fletcher challenged the Mar Dive Group's "arrest" of the wreck. The Ontario court found the California court had no jurisdiction over the matter, stating, "Taking all the factors into consideration, it is my view that the U.S. judgments were obtained by means of half-truths and artificiality. As such, I would have found that the U.S. judgments ought not to be recognized and enforced in this jurisdiction as they are against public policy."

So pretty much all of the salvagers' attempts to find treasure turned out to be failures. Except perhaps for Mike Fletcher, who viewed the site as a source of riches of a more philosophical bent. Now protected by the courts, the wreck remains at the bottom of the lake, and the recovered items are being returned to the Province of Ontario.

Fast ferry fast update — *plus ça change*

Update: In the original *Colossal Canadian Failures*, we told you the story of the so-called fast ferry program. Called "They're slow and they cost a lot," the piece was about the idea of the British Columbia government to build a faster, lighter, more comfortable ferry for speedy commuter service along the coast and among the islands of British Columbia. Three ships would be delivered in three years to B.C. Ferries. And if the design was good enough, the west coast shipbuilding industry could expand to meet the demands of the orders that would inevitably flow in from around the world.

It was a wonderful idea. But, as our book noted, in reality, the ferries were slower than planned, more expensive, and much less comfortable. And the orders have not exactly been flooding in.

Just for fun, here is a partial list of the table of contents for the report on the fast ferry from the province's auditor general, George Morfit, which was delivered in October 1999:

- Fast ferries were not shown to be the best way to meet identified needs.

- The risks inherent in the fast ferry project were never adequately identified.

- The likelihood that fast aluminum ferries could be built cost-effectively in British Columbia was not demonstrated.

- The likelihood of exporting British Columbia–built fast ferries was not demonstrated.

- The costs announced were not well-supported.

- A realistic budget and firm control on the scope of changes were never established.

- The schedule for the project was never announced.

- An overriding concern with meeting the unrealistic schedule meant that work was rushed and some-times done out of sequence.

- The designer and design were chosen before B.C. Ferries' operational needs were fully defined.

- Construction was started before detailed engineer-ing work was sufficiently complete.

- B.C. Ferries board was pressed into a hurried decision.

- B.C. Ferries board repeatedly tried to obtain more information as the project progressed.

- Accountability reporting to the Legislative Assembly and public was inadequate.

And according to the auditor general, it was unrealistic to expect even shipyards familiar with the construction of fast ferries to design and build three craft so quickly.

The boondoggle took another turn for the weird in 2003. The ferries were sold, all three, for the bargain basement price of $20 million Canadian.

It cost about $450 million to build them. When it was time to sell, they were valued at $70 million. It's estimated that the price they were sold at was equivalent to the scrap value of the aluminum hulls. Apparently an anonymous North American bidder picked up the three catamarans. Perhaps they're going to be recycled into the world's coolest, fastest beer cans.

The former NDP government commissioned the ships, then blasted the sale. Gordon Wilson, a former NDP cabinet minister, said, "State of the art vessels being sold for scrap value is a much bigger scandal than building them in the first place."

Not surprisingly, Liberal B.C. Premier Gordon Campbell defended the sale, saying the fast ferries program was a "debacle" and they simply should never have been built in the first place. Campbell admitted the price paid for the fast ferries was like something out of a flea market fantasy but said his government's job was to try to minimize the losses from the program.

So in order to minimize the losses to the province, he sold the boats, which cost $450 million, for $20 million. Now that's minimizing.

"Advance! Um, or not."

You can change the name of a ship, but you can't change its destiny.

The *Sir S.L. Tilley* was built in 1884 by L. Shickluna in St. Catharines, Ontario. It was pretty tough. Shickluna built ships that plied the waters of the Great Lakes for decades and were highly thought of by those who knew boats.

Unfortunately, the *Tilley* soon had a captain that apparently lacked certain navigational skills. In 1889, he was sailing along the Detroit River and managed to sail right into the lighthouse at the river's mouth.

Surviving that debacle, the ship managed to remain relatively accident-free for ten years, until the night of August 26, 1899. That night, while she was heading to Cleveland to load coal, a fire started in the engine room.

It soon spread. The engineer and fifteen others jumped into a boat that took them safely to a schooner that happened to be in town.

The engineer left the engine on full speed ahead, so the poor wheelsman and a deckhand remained aboard steering the burning vessel toward Fairport. They finally gave up and jumped into the lake, where a steamer picked them up.

The blazing *Tilley* ran aground, burned up and sank.

The insurance underwriter refloated the hull and sold it to Bingley & Son Ltd. in Cornwall, Ontario. Now called the *Advance*, the ship was put back in service to run coal from Toronto to ports along lakes Erie and Ontario.

The *Advance* soon got a reputation for crashing into things in the Welland Canal, including a swing bridge.

There are several versions of her last days. Our favourite, if only because it would be typical, involves yet another collision. In December 1927, long after most ships were off the lakes, the *Advance* crashed into the rocks off Manitoulin Island.

Although the ship itself seemed to know its fate, the owners again salvaged her. But they too realized that the *Advance* had run out its days and declared it a total loss.

Canal and lighthouse keepers throughout the Great Lakes likely cheered.

Maybe they put it up there to keep it away from the *Advance*

Look up.

Look way up.

No, higher.

Way, way, way up.

Look up about 190 metres.

That's how high above sea level the Triangle Island lighthouse was.

That's pretty high for a lighthouse.

Oh, it was a good lighthouse — the federal government saw to that. The government had a highly polished, light-magnifying fresnel lens brought in by ship and hauled up the steep hill, and then it constructed a heavy base to hold the mercury bath to float the lens in. Tonnes of concrete were hauled up and reinforced with steel to form the base on which the lantern structure was erected, all at the cost of a small fortune.

But the federal government erected this triumph of technology at the top of the island's spine, with awkward results.

First, the hurricane-force winds at the top of the island were a constant problem, tearing away at the lighthouse and regularly damaging it. The wind was so bad that it once blew a lighthouse keeper's dog off the summit.

Second, it was high, very high. A great place for a lighthouse, you'd think. You'd be wrong. On Triangle Island, just north of Vancouver

Photograph by Don Waite, Waite Air Photos Inc.

Triangle Island is a rocky ridge jutting from the Pacific Ocean just north of Vancouver Island. At the summit, just visible is a small bump, which is the foundation of the old lighthouse.

Island, it's often pretty cloudy at that height. Even without the clouds, sailors weren't used to looking that high for the guiding beacon of a lighthouse. By the time anyone could see the Triangle Island lighthouse, they'd be so close to the island's ragged, rocky shores that they'd be looking up from their sinking ship, fixing to die.

The Triangle Island lighthouse was erected in 1910. Only eight years later, it was decommissioned. Today, it makes a nice display at the Sooke Region Museum, safe and sound on the mainland, where it can do no harm.

You call it a bridge, I call it a hazard

It seems obvious. When you build a bridge that ships have to go under, you put the part the ships have to go under over the deepest water. That way the ships can safely manoeuvre under your bridge.

That should have been done for the bridge built over the channel known as the Second Narrows in Burrard Inlet in British Columbia. Shipping experts warned the Burret Inlet Tunnel and Bridge Company to put the lift span over the centre of the channel where the water is deepest. To save money, the company built the lift span at the bridge's south end. The water wasn't as deep there.

On November 3, 1925, the Second Narrows Bridge was opened. It seemed to be a success, with three thousand cars crossing on opening day.

Then the ships started to come through. When they tried to make it under the span where the water was shallow, they hit the bridge with alarming regularity.

No one was severely hurt or killed in the accidents, but the bridge got the nickname the Bridge of Sighs.

Only five years after it opened, in April 1930, a ship called the *Losmar* crashed into the south span, tearing part of the structure away. In September, the *Pacific Gatherer* came up the inlet and took out the centre span. The bridge was closed. The Burrard Inlet Tunnel and Bridge Company went bankrupt. A new bridge was eventually built, but not before the government appointed a commission to investigate what went wrong with the old one.

In only five years, dozens of vessels "came into contact with the bridge," the commission reported a year later.

Six accidents involved deep-sea vessels and four caused heavy damage. The bridge was consistent in taking its toll among larger ships: the *Eurana* in 1927, the *Norwich City* in 1928, the *Losmar* in 1930, and the *Pacific Gatherer* in 1930.

After the *Eurana* crashed, the Burrard Inlet Tunnel and Bridge Company had the nerve to sue the vessel's owners for damage to the bridge. After all, the bridge couldn't move out of the way, but the *Eurana* could have.

City of Vancouver Archives, Br P9.

City of Vancouver Archives, CVA 99-2151

In 1930, the Second Narrows Bridge took a double knockout that shut it down for good. In April the *Losmar* of the Calmar Line (TOP) knocked down a span of the bridge. In September, the *Pacific Gatherer* smacked into the bridge and had to be pulled out by the tug *Lorne* (BOTTOM).

The owners of the *Eurana* countered-sued for $77,000. Two levels of court threw out both claims, but the final word went to the Privy Council in England.

The council ruled against the bridge company, saying its daftly designed structure was a "substantial interference with navigation amounting to a public nuisance."

And we could ship beer in a giant beer can ship

If only Britain had some gumption, Canada would be a world leader today in making a product that changed the world.

Back in the early 1820s, the British government put a timber tax on oak and pine. As if living in a land filled with snow half the year and mosquitoes the other half wasn't hard enough, Britain was now taxing one of the few enterprises in which a colonist could make a decent living.

The colonial masters, though, underestimated the colonists' ingenuity. A man named Macpherson realized that a ship could be built of squared timbers pegged together. There was no tax on ships. The ship could be sailed across the ocean then taken apart in Britain. Voila, squared timber, delivered to Britain in the guise of a ship, with no tax.

Historian J.J. Brown writes that the first disposable ship, the 3,690-ton *Columbus*, made the voyage to England in 1824. The darn thing worked so well that the shipbuilders didn't dismantle it. Instead, the *Columbus* returned to Quebec City and headed again to England. Then something happened. The *Columbus* ran into a storm and sank.

Even so, another ship was being built. She was 304 feet long and displaced 5,294 tons. This ship made the voyage to England and was there broken up for the timber.

The plan had worked! Canada would soon be known the world over for building disposable ships. The possibilities were endless. Ships made of beaver skins. Ships made of cod. And generations later, ships made of car parts, ships made of CANDU reactors. And every ship easily taken apart. Who needed to build expensive ships to carry things when you could make the ships out of the things themselves? The cost of goods everywhere would drop. There'd be an end to world hunger.

Then the Brits came to their senses and abolished the tax. A great Canadian initiative — disposed of.

CHAPTER 3

CANALS AND TRAINS

What's more efficient, shipping goods by canal or by train? That was the big debate in Canada for much of the 1800s and the early part of the 1900s. Some entrepreneurs answered the question with their schemes. The conclusion? Neither.

If I stayed another year in Canada, they'd want me to build a bloody railway

William Baillie-Grohman was a big game hunter, adventurer, and entrepreneur with an English jolliness and dry British wit that he turned toward the wilderness of British Columbia in the 1880s. For fifteen years he had adventures and misadventures in the Kootenay region. But nothing tried his inner strength more than digging a small ditch between two lakes.

"As a test of temper and of perseverance against the forces of nature, the malignity of man, and the cussedness of fate, there is, I can assure the reader, nothing like building in a wild uninhabited country, far removed from civilized means of transportation, a canal according to plans imposed upon you by people who have never been to the spot and who have no conception of what is really required," he wrote years later.

In some ways, he should have known better. In 1884, Baillie-Grohman was granted thirty thousand acres of land in Lower Kootenay. In return, he was supposed to obtain a steamer to service the Lower Kootenay River and Lake Kootenay. He found one in Norway and had it shipped to Montreal. That was the easy part. In Montreal, customs officials wanted to charge him a high tariff for bringing the steamer into the country. Baillie-Grohman didn't want to pay any tariff on a steamer he was being forced to bring into the country. Even then, Canada was getting a reputation for having a bloated bureaucracy.

"The amount and rigidness of red tape that manacles the official world of Canada is something incredible," he recalled. Unable to convince customs officials not to impose the tariff, Baillie-Grohman took his case to a cabinet minister in Ottawa. The enterprising Brit pointed out that agricultural machinery was tariff-free. Since most of the land he was about to get was underwater half the year, he argued, the steamer should count as farm equipment and be tariff-free. Red tape there may have been in Canada, but there was an equally strong sense of humour, and the amused minister waived the tariff.

Once the steamer was shipped by CPR to the nearest station, Baillie-Grohman hired men to pull and roll the steamer by tackle, pulley, and logs over a pass in the Selkirk Mountains to the Kootenay River. The antiquated engine had already been taken out and left behind in Duluth, Minnesota, but it still took three weeks to move the hull sixty-five kilometres through the bush. The steamer, called the *Midge*, did a fine job on the river and lake, and Baillie-Grohman turned his mind to his next project.

In the wild and circuitous way of rivers in mountains, at one point the source of the Columbia River, Columbia Lake, is only two kilometres away from the Kootenay River. All that separates the two river systems is a flat sandy plain. Baillie-Grohman's land in the Lower Kootenay valley was rich and fertile grassland in spring and fall, but in summer, as water poured from the mountains and the river rose, his grassland became swamps and lakes. He sought approval from British Columbia to dig a ditch up where the Kootenay River swung close to Columbia Lake so that the water from the river would rush into the lake and the Columbia River system. That way his land farther down the river would be spared the flooding of meltwater each summer. It was only returning the river to its original path, Baillie-Grohman figured, because surely the Kootenay at one time must have flowed over the flat. Besides, eventually the Kootenay does join up with the Columbia — just farther downstream.

Surprisingly enough, or perhaps not, considering the nature of B.C. politics, Baillie-Grohman got initial approval to divert one giant river system into another. Unfortunately for him and fortunately for the B.C. wilderness, Baillie-Grohman's initial approval came from the province. Apparently, he learned later, it had no authority to give that approval. Canal-building came under the federal government's jurisdiction.

Besides that, between the time he first cooked up the idea in 1882 and two years later when it was first approved, people had moved into the valley between the two source lakes, inconveniently inhabiting the land that would have been flooded.

Equally importantly, the railway was headed into the Columbia Valley. Railway surveyors planned on building the tracks above the high-water mark of the Columbia River and "did not consider the possibility of vast volumes of water being added to that of the Columbia," Baillie-Grohman noted.

The CPR learned of the proposed water diversion and urged the federal government to quash the plans. As Baillie-Grohman wryly noted, the federal government relied so heavily on the railway's success for its political fortunes that the red tape so cumbersome to others was promptly unravelled and the railway got its way.

But Baillie-Grohman got another deal. If he would build a canal on the flatland, which he called Canal Flat, he could have thirty thousand acres of land in the Upper Kootenay region.

"It would have been better if I had abandoned the whole scheme at this stage," he recalled. The new canal wasn't going to do anything to stop the flooding because it would not be open during high water. It cost about twenty times the amount of his original plan to turn the river permanently into the Columbia. And the design demanded by the federal government suggested to the Brit that the proposed canal itself would do little to help navigation between the two rivers. However, he had already invested thousands of pounds in the scheme. And he was going to get thirty thousand acres of higher, drier land. So he signed the deal in 1887 with a two-year deadline.

One of the first steps was to build a steam sawmill at Canal Flat to cut the wood for the lock and lockworks. After convincing an eastern supplier to sell him a mill to be shipped out west, Baillie-Grohman next had to, as he put it, "wheedle ... the mighty arbitrator out West, i.e. the head of the freight department of the Canadian Pacific Railroad."

The head of the freight department, more powerful than almost any politician, deigned to meet Baillie-Grohman in Montreal and after some haggling agreed to ship the sawmill parts at a rate only slightly damaging to Baillie-Grohman's pocket book.

"Your heart is filled with gratitude that the great line, built with the people's money, deigns to handle your poor little freight at all," the ever-wry Baillie-Grohman noted.

The machinery was shipped to Golden, B.C., in August and unloaded, at Baillie-Grohman's expense and effort, beside the tracks, where it sat for weeks because of the rain, under guard, also at Baillie-Grohman's expense, because lifting unguarded railway goods was simply too tempting for some scoundrels to resist.

Despite the rain, the Columbia River had fallen to its typical late summer low. The one steamer on the river, the only boat capable of pulling a five-thousand-pound sawmill to Canal Flat, had grounded and eventually sank.

Fortunately, or so it seemed at the time, an enterprising man had decided to put a rival steamer on the river and bought a more or less square barge used in railway construction.

The new steamer, the *Cline*, had a few nautical flaws. With an almost square shape and a small stern wheel, she preferred to head up the river sideways rather than the more traditional way, bow first. The boiler, taken from a steam plough in Manitoba, was built to handle coal. There was no coal on the banks of the Columbia, so the crew of eight had to cut wood "to about the size of grown up toothpicks," Baillie-Grohman said. Then the toothpicks had to be soaked in coal oil, so the fire would generate steam to run the engine.

Built of four-inch planks, the *Cline* was too heavy to carry the sawmill boiler, so the boiler was placed on a raft and towed. That sawmill boiler was the only dry place on the boat, so Baillie-Grohman claimed it for his sleeping quarters. Up the Columbia the *Cline* went, past submerged tree trunks and sandbars, occasionally heading into a channel in a swamp only to find it was a dead end. The *Cline* got stuck on one sandbar and half the cargo had to be taken off before the crew, in waist deep and chilly water, could pry the boat over the bar. As they worked, rustlers helped themselves to what they could of the cargo. Baillie-Grohman went back days later to look for some of the missing goods and came across a stack of what he thought was another poor victim's load, dumped until the river rose again and the steamer could pass. Hungry, he helped himself to some beans. Then he checked the bag to see whose beans he had eaten. Turns out the bag of beans was his own, stolen and dumped earlier.

The hundred-mile trip up the Columbia took twenty-three days.

The sawmill and machinery in place, Baillie-Grohman dug the canal. It was not much more than a big ditch, he recalled, 6,700 feet long and 45 feet wide. Building the locks and floodgates turned out to be a lot trickier. Because the 100-foot-long, 30-foot-wide lock had to be sunk so deep, deeper than the level of the Kootenay, water seeped into the excavations. Steam pumps had to be shipped in from the coast. The on-site government engineer, paid for by the month by Baillie-Grohman, was no help. Finally they finished the lock at the Columbia end of the canal, and a wooden guard gate was built at the Kootenay end.

"Thus it came to pass that, in defiance of reason and common sense, the works had to be completed at the cost of sums which might as well have been thrown into the sea," the new canal builder lamented.

The canal was completed in 1889, within the two-year deadline.

Within twelve months, the canal was shut down.

According to Baillie-Grohman, the government suddenly grew worried that the Kootenay could overflow the lock and flow into the Columbia. That, he pointed out, was exactly what he was trying to do in the first place.

Other accounts suggest the canal was used, perhaps after Baillie-Grohman gave up and returned to Europe. One large steamer came through in 1894. Another steamer, the *North Star*, arrived at the canal sometime in 1902, but it was too big to fit into the locks. Only by building new dams and destroying the old lock and gate was the *North Star* able to go through the canal. That was the second and last steamer to use the canal.

By then Baillie-Grohman was back in Europe and happy to be home.

One ditch away from industrial greatness

One town's dream to become a commercial powerhouse on Lake Ontario through the use of canals led to a railway disaster and not much else.

The community of Dundas, near Hamilton, sits only eight kilometres from a body of water called Cootes Paradise, which in turn leads to Burlington Bay on the western end of Lake Ontario. In 1825, six straightforward Dundas men founded the straightforwardly named Canal Corporation.

The little canal they planned would give Dundas access to huge markets on the Great Lakes, on both sides of the border. An Act of Parliament in 1826 approved the canal, with a maximum cost of £10,000. Of course, by 1837, the original £10,000 was gone and the government had handed out another £17,000. It didn't seem to matter. Simply in anticipation of a canal being built, at least a dozen businesses sprang up in Dundas.

By the time the canal opened on August 16, 1837, Dundas boasted two carriage factories, a sawmill, a cabinet factory, two brickyards, two chair factories, four hotels, three doctor's offices, an axe foundry, a newspaper, and two breweries. Cannon blasts, music, fireworks, and a dance marked the opening of the canal.

Prosperity was right around the corner.

In Hamilton.

It turned out the Desjardins Canal, named after the man who first dreamed it up, didn't have enough water for the really large vessels operating in the lakes.

But Hamilton had lots of water. And Hamilton also had a railway. So Dundas decided it had better get railway service too.

The Canal Corporation built a swing bridge over the canal, at a cost of £10,000, in order for trains to travel into Dundas. The swing bridge opened on January 5, 1854. Less than three years later, on March 16, 1857, a train carrying ninety passengers headed into Hamilton from Toronto and crossed the swing bridge. The train derailed and fell twenty metres into the frozen canal. Only twenty people survived. That bridge was never rebuilt. Ten years later a sandbar developed across the mouth of the canal.

Hamilton became an industrial powerhouse. Dundas became a pretty town where many Hamilton workers live. The Desjardins Canal draws no large ships, but it does attract plenty of canoes.

Made in Canada and stayed in Canada

Two long waterways opened up Ontario and Western Canada to the East. The northern route, popular with fur traders, explorers, and Jesuits, took travellers up the Ottawa River to the Mattawa River and then up to Trout Lake in Northern Ontario. One four-mile portage later, travellers entered the Vase River, which drained into Lake Nippissing, which drained via the French River into Georgian Bay. Voila! The West was now yours to explore. And the route, not lost on military leaders, was all in Canada.

The southern route is three hundred miles longer. Down the St. Lawrence to Lake Ontario, then up and around those bloody Niagara Falls, then Lake St. Clair, and finally Lake Huron.

Library and Archives Canada/
C-022118

The junction of the Ottawa and Mattawa rivers was photographed circa 1905 to support efforts to build a canal from Ottawa through the wilderness to Georgian Bay. After $500,000 in studies and a lot of political wrangling, the government chose the route that made sense, along the St. Lawrence and the Great Lakes, where people actually lived.

Although the route is longer, in some ways it was easier for explorers and traders to travel. Aside from the one big drop at Niagara, it offered fewer rapids.

It's no wonder that when canal fever hit Canada in the 1800s, a battle began over the best route to build canals to the West: the Ottawa River route or the St. Lawrence route.

The first survey of the Ottawa route, made in 1856, put the cost at $24 million. Three years later, another proposal put the cost at $12 million. A Royal Commission was struck and concluded it couldn't figure out anything because the two figures were so vastly different. No matter, in 1884 the Montreal, Ottawa and Georgian Bay Canal Company was created. Two years later a Senate committee gave its approval of an Ottawa–Georgian Bay canal, and an English canal contractor stepped up and agreed to build the canal if financing was put in place.

As effective then as the Senate is today, nothing happened. The century turned, the portages up the Ottawa and Lakes routes remained. Finally, in 1904 the federal government commissioned a new survey of the Ottawa route. The government put aside $250,000 for the survey. About $500,000 later the six-hundred-page "Report upon the Survey for the Georgian Bay Ship Canal, with Plans and Estimates of Cost, 1908," came out. The engineers concluded that a twenty-two-foot-wide waterway could be built for $100 million. It would take a lake freight boat travelling twelve miles an hour seventy hours to go from Montreal to Georgian Bay, one to one and a half days faster than the Great Lakes route.

The detailed report, made after much hard work, seemed to turn the tide to the Ottawa–Georgian Bay canal. Sir Wilfrid Laurier, running for re-election in 1911, supported the all-in-Canada route.

Unfortunately for the Ottawa–Georgian Bay supporters, Laurier lost that election to Sir Robert Borden. The costs of the First World War stalled the project even further. By the time the war ended, railways had taken over from canals as the major transportation routes. Sure, Canada still needed a shipping lane to the West. But the Ottawa route, officials noticed, also contained a lot of waterfalls that could be used to generate power. They also noted that a lot more people lived in a lot more cities along the Great Lakes than along the Ottawa and French rivers. Why put a canal in the northern wilderness when the markets and factories were already based in the south? The Montreal, Ottawa and Georgian Bay Canal Company lost its charter in 1927, ending the dream of an all-Canadian route linking the East to the West.

Keep your railway away from our railway

Railways, *chemins de fer*, the ribbons of steel that bind us as Canadians, are romantic things.

And sometimes silly, not-so-romantic things happened while they were being built.

Like when Edmonton railroaders were trying to push out of that northern Alberta city with the embryonic Edmonton, Yukon and Pacific Railway.

Ahh, sounds grand, doesn't it? In reality, it almost died before it got started, and it was really a failure of the competition to keep it "off track" that allowed it to live.

Tootle along with us and take a sojourn along the mighty EY&P.

The EY&P started off humbly enough as the Edmonton District Railway. That name sounds more suitable for an organization like a school board or a chamber of commerce. Just because you tack "railway" onto the end doesn't make it a railway. And apparently it wasn't much of a railway to begin with.

In 1896, it had been given the charter to send forth steely tendrils to Strathcona and points north. Places like St. Albert and Fort Saskatchewan. By 1899, it had been reorganized into the grander sounding EY&P. Then, it became part of the even grander sounding Canadian Northern Railway, a much more national-sounding name. Canadian Northern was in Manitoba, laying track towards Alberta. Adding EY&P gave it an immediate presence farther west.

But back in Alberta, Edmonton was facing railroad rivalry from nearby Strathcona. Edmonton was a boomtown thanks to the gold rush, but Strathcona wound up being designated the northern terminus of the Canadian Pacific Railway. The gravy train had come to Strathcona, and the good people of Strathcona liked it that way.

So imagine their dismay when Edmonton's EY&P (part of CPR's rival, the Canadian National Railway) got permission from the federal government in 1902 to link with the CPR line in, wait for it, Strathcona. Their rivals in Edmonton were being allowed to tap into their railway line with a rival line. And if EY&P could throw its rail line past the CPR line and reach into the north, the new-found wealth Strathcona was experiencing would be threatened.

The EY&Pers stretched north with their rail. Finally, on November 8, 1902, EY&P's rail line was ready to be connected to the CPR line. But Strathcona was ready, too. A constable from Strathcona, apparently uncaring that the federal government had granted permission for this connection, threatened to throw the EY&P workers in jail if they tried even touching the rail line. A rather large gathering of Strathconians, apparently equally uncaring, was there to back him up.

Soon a switch engine — that's a tiny locomotive — arrived from the Strathcona rail yard and began running back and forth over the stretch of track the EY&P crew needed to link into in order to cross the line. It's difficult to pull up track in order to put in a switch and connect everything back up again with a train running back and forth over the track that needs pulling up. It's actually kind of dangerous.

So the rail line crew of EY&P sent word back to Edmonton, and by the early afternoon a good-sized contingent of Edmontonians was on hand at the challenged rail site.

The switch engine rattled back and forth, and as the smoke cleared from its engine at each pass, the crowds for the two communities continued to eye each other in as aggressive a manner as an eyeing can take.

The standoff might have lasted forever, but at 5:25 p.m. a messenger from the Strathcona rail yard arrived to inform the switch engine that it would have to clear the tracks so the evening northbound train could get through. So the little engine sputtered down the tracks, home to the Strathcona yards. The train from Calgary rumbled past shortly after it.

As soon as it was out of sight, the work gang from Edmonton ran onto the vacated tracks. Surrounded by the Edmonton crowd, the crew ripped out some track, plopped in a switch and crossed the line. Edmonton was connected by rail to the outside world.

Long names, short rides

For a while in the 1800s and early 1900s, it seemed any group of men with a bit of money could get together, charter a railway company, and propose a line with a grandiose name guaranteed to attract more investors.

It was a given that a solid railway company had to have the word *Great* in its name. *Transcontinental* was another good word to throw in.

Whatever the promoters called their railways, Canadians developed a knack for even better nicknames.

The Pacific Great Eastern Railway, started in 1912, was supposed to take trains from Vancouver to Prince George, B.C. But delays in building were frequent and it took until the 1950s to get the rail line completed. Naturally, the PGE soon stood for Prince George Eventually and Past God's Endurance.

Soon after the Port Arthur, Duluth and Western Railway opened in the 1890s, the silver market in northwestern Ontario collapsed, throwing hundreds of miners out of work. The railway became known as the Poverty, Agony, Distress and Want Railway.

Perhaps it was a comment on the cities involved, but the Toronto Hamilton Buffalo Railway in southern Ontario was nicknamed To Hell and Back.

Hundreds of railroads were promoted but never got built. And some that did get built shouldn't have. Perhaps the shortest lived railway was the one at Stokes Bay, Ontario, built in about 1880.

Stokes Bay is on Tamarac Island in Ontario's Georgian Bay. The forests on the island prompted the building of a sawmill. In order to bring wood from the forests to the mill, the mill owner built a railroad.

Given he had trees to spare, the owner built the tracks out of wood. On its very first trip, the engine split the tracks and derailed. That was the first and last trip of the Stokes Bay Railway — excuse us, the Great Transcontinental Georgian Bay Railway Company.

CHAPTER 4

AIR TRAVEL

Except during snowstorms, Canadians have always looked up to the sky and dreamed. In parts of the country, there's nothing else to look at anyway.

Do we fall slower in metric?

As Canada prepared to go metric in the early seventies, pundits and ordinary people predicted disaster. Generations of Canadians raised on the British imperial system of measurement — the pounds and inches of the past — would not be able to adapt.

Supporters said the country had to go metric because the U.S. was going to make the switch to kilograms and kilometres. The U.S. never did go metric, once again proving we should never try to follow its lead on anything.

In a typically Canadian way, our country compromised on metric. Speeds and weights of food are in metric. Temperatures are in metric, though half the country probably still converts to Fahrenheit to know for sure how cold it really is outside. Weights and heights of people remain firmly in the imperial system. Building materials use both systems. It hasn't been a disaster, but there was almost a disaster because of it.

On July 23, 1983, a Boeing 767, Aircraft 604, carrying sixty-one passengers and eight crew members, was preparing to take off from Montreal for Edmonton. There were problems with an on-board computer, called the fuel quantity processor, which tells the cockpit crew how much fuel the plane has. As a result, the fuel gauges were blank. That meant the ground crew had to gauge the fuel by the old-fashioned method called the drip or dip. The method was similar to checking the oil in a car. Once the crew knew how much fuel was left in the plane's tank, they would simply add the right amount of fuel. Then that amount would be put into another computer, called the flight management computer, to show the pilots how much fuel was left as the plane was flying.

Flight 143 needed 22,300 kilograms to fly from Montreal to Edmonton, without refuelling in Ottawa. The fuel was pumped in by a truck that measured the outgoing fuel in volume, in litres. But the fuel in the tanks was measured in weight, in kilograms. To convert from litres, the volume, to kilograms, the weight, involved a relatively simple formula that everyone knew: multiply the number of litres by 1.77.

Unfortunately, the formula everyone knew was used to convert litres to imperial pounds. That's the formula everyone had been using for the rest of the planes, which still measured weight in pounds. They should have multiplied by 0.8209.

An imperial pound is about half the weight of a kilogram. That meant the refuelling crews had actually put in only half the amount of fuel they thought they had.

The figures were punched into the flight management computer — 22,600 kilograms of fuel, plenty to get to Edmonton.

In fact, when the jet took off, it had 22,600 pounds of fuel, or less than 10,000 kilograms.

Some of the flight crew and ground crew were uneasy about the calculations. Just to make sure, another drip was made and figures rechecked in Ottawa. Then the numbers were put again into the flight management computer. Up in the air the new 767 went.

Just over Red Lake, Ontario, a warning buzzer beeped four times. There was something wrong with the left forward fuel pump. That wasn't a huge problem. The two wing tanks and one belly tank were connected by pipes. If the left fuel pump failed, the crew could simply feed the left engine from the other tanks. Another four beeps sounded. The second left fuel pump was failing. Captain Bob Pearson decided to head straight to Winnipeg.

Five minutes later, eight more beeps sounded. All six pumps in all three tanks were failing. Four minutes after that, the cockpit crew heard a sharp bong. The left engine was gone. Still, landing a jet on one engine was quite doable.

Then things got really bad. The entire cockpit display went blank. The lights went out. The 767 used jet fuel to turn two engines that ran the generators that ran the entire computer system in the cockpit. If there was no fuel, then there was nothing to run the on-board computer system. But of course there was fuel, right?

No. It became painfully clear to the shocked crew that the problem wasn't bad pumps. The pumps had no fuel to pump. Amidst all the beeps and bongs one can hear on the cockpit recorder, quite audibly and quite intelligibly, First Officer Maurice Quintal saying "Holy f——."

That was an understatement. Not only was the plane out of the fuel that made it go, it was also out of the fuel that supplied emergency electrical and pneumatic power needed to control the plane. Fortunately, an emergency backup system had been installed. A small propeller opened up on the side of the plane. The propeller used the speed of the plane to turn a generator that fed a hydraulic pump, just enough to run the plane's hydraulic controls.

The crew quickly checked the manuals to see what to do next in the case of two engines failing at once. There was nothing in the manual. Not even an appropriate prayer.

Nor had the pilots been trained what to do. They had to think quickly.

The 767 began sinking so fast, they knew it would never make Winnipeg. However, only about twelve kilometres away was an abandoned Royal Canadian Air Force Base in Gimli. The base had been abandoned but the twin 6,800-foot runways remained.

Spotting the air base's old approach towers, Pearson started his approach. Unfortunately, the towers guided him not to the right runway, which was still used by small planes, but to the left runway, which had been turned into a dragstrip, with a steel guardrail installed to divide it into two drag racing lanes. The good news was that drag racing was not taking place that day. The bad news was that it was Family Day for the Winnipeg Sports Car Club. Kids were playing and parents were relaxing beside campers and barbecues after an earlier rally.

Meanwhile, the 767 dropped below radar and the crew suddenly learned that the propeller-driven hydraulic system didn't operate the landing gear. So the pilots tried to operate it manually, using the force of the wind to drop the gear into place. The nose gear didn't lock. Coming in too high and too fast, Pearson executed a manoeuvre called a sideslip, which drops the plane sickeningly fast. The plane shot toward the runway at 180 knots, about 50 knots faster than normal. A few people on the runway looked up. The same words that Quintal spoke in the cockpit were repeated on the ground.

The plane hit the runway and Pearson stood on the brakes. Two tires blew out, racing fans screamed and fled, the nose gear collapsed, and the nose scraped and bounced along the tarmac. Fewer than thirty metres from the spectators, the 767 — sparks flying from its nose as it scraped and bounced on the runway — came to a stop. Passengers applauded, but when a fire broke out in the nose, flight attendants ushered them out the rear emergency slides. Because the nose was down, it was a steep ride out and some passengers were hurt. Those were the only injuries. Some Car Club members put out the fire with handheld extinguishers.

An internal investigation by Air Canada determined that Captain Bob Pearson, First Officer Maurice Quintal, and three mechanics were to blame for the crash. An independent board of inquiry, though, concluded there was a series of mistakes made throughout Air Canada and absolved the flight crew and mechanics.

A key mistake: pushing the metric system through too quickly. Under pressure from the federal government, Air Canada had purchased new aircraft that measured fuel in kilograms. All the other planes still used the imperial system of pounds and no one was trained properly in the metric system.

The plane became known as the Gimli Glider. Aside from hundreds of thousands of headaches from parents caught between their imperial education and their children's metric education, the Gimli Glider remains the most notable metric system victim.

And it may be backwoods legend, but the story goes that when mechanics were sent from Winnipeg Airport to repair the plane, they ran out of gas. It's not clear how they calculated *their* fuel load.

What if we piled all the reports in the water? That might fill the gap.

It's just under one hundred metres wide, a warm-up dip for a long-distance swimmer, a leisurely drift in a canoe.

Yet after seventy years of effort, involving dozens of proposals, no one has yet been able to float an idea, bridge a gap in opposing arguments, or tunnel through red tape to put a fixed link between Toronto and a little island airport just to the south of the city.

Originally, there was no problem getting to the Toronto Islands because there were no islands, just a nine-kilometre-long peninsula attached to the mainland. Storms in 1852 turned the spit into an island. Harbour authorities filled in the eastern end, without a single task force, joint committee, or consultant involved.

The take-on again, take-off again airport

Could someone just make a decision, please?

Back in 1972, the Ontario and federal governments decided to build a second international airport near Pickering, Ontario, to ease the strain on Pearson International Airport, as it's called now, near Malton.

The governments expropriated 7,300 hectares and kicked 1,300 people off their land. A group called People or Planes protested; they didn't want an international airport next to their homes. In 1975 the federal government backed down. Four years later, a report by federal and provincial transport officials declared the project officially dead.

In 1982, a group that eventually became known as the Green Door Alliance recommended that the airport land be returned to private hands. Nothing happened.

Seven years later, Pearson became so crowded that the federal government again raised the prospect of building an airport at Pickering. Nothing happened.

In 1998, local politicians tried to resurrect the airport. The federal government declared the area a "major airport site." Nothing happened.

In 2004, the Greater Toronto Airports Authority announced its latest plans to build a $2-billion airport in Pickering. By the fall of 2005, protests against the airport were mounting.

The Airports Authority plan is subject to federal government approval, environmental assessments, and public consultations. In any case, the Airports Authority said, construction and expansion would take place over the next twenty-eight years.

That would mean the airport would be completed, at the earliest, by 2032 — a mere sixty years after the plan was first announced.

Six years later the spit was breached again, and this time the eastern gap was so deep and wide that steamers could get in. So everyone left it as is. The islands were now a part of Toronto life.

Unfortunately, sediment kept filling in the western channel. So in 1910, the federal government dredged a new western channel. Yes, this is the same western channel that everyone has spent the past seventy years trying to bridge.

Even as the government was finishing up the dredging, the first plan to connect the island floated to the surface. A Parks Department commissioner proposed a sixteen-foot-wide pedestrian and automobile tunnel to connect to a new road for the island. That idea sank but was dredged up again in 1913, when the federal government agreed to build two bridges, one for the Eastern Gap and one for the Western Gap, to connect the proposed island roadway to the mainland. Then someone pointed out that the steamers would knock into the bridges. The idea was scrapped.

The federal government decided in 1935 to create jobs by spending $1 million to build a tunnel under the gap. Work was started, the government fell, and work was cancelled.

Meanwhile, people started flying seaplanes to the islands. In 1937, politicians decided to build a municipal airport on the islands. They also decided to put one near Malton, as a backup in case of fog. The backup is now the huge Pearson International Airport.

With what was supposed to be the city's main airport stuck on an island, proposals to link the island to the mainland surfaced in 1948, 1956, 1957, 1958, 1960 (six in that year alone), 1961, 1962, 1963, and … well, the interest was fairly consistent by then.

The ideas ranged from one-lane tunnels to a cableway, with the prices ranging from a mere $263,000 for the cableway to $6 million for a two-lane tunnel.

A consultant's report in 1965 recommended that a two-lane tunnel, for buses only, be dug from the mainland at Bathurst Street all the way under the channel and under the airport runways to a terminal building. The cost of $9.9 million, with $80,250 a year in operating costs, would be worth it to avoid stagnation of the Island Airport and to allow it to realize its full potential.

That rallying cry was to be used for the next forty years.

Through the late sixties and the seventies the ideas just kept flowing. On average, from 1965 to 1975 there was one idea per year. Some visionaries proposed building a $5-billion floating airport several kilometres into Lake Ontario, serviced by a helicopters or hovercraft or, if that was impractical, a subway tunnel suspended fifty feet below the surface of lake. The airport would float on hollow concrete boxes in four hundred feet of water. The boxes could turn the runways so planes could always land into the wind. A second, smaller, floating airport could be built to handle commuter traffic.

Somewhat saner minds turned back to the gap. Why build a floating airport when an island airport already existed?

Finally, by 1975, it appeared the little gap was going to be filled, come hell or high water. The airport's operations were unprofitable, so the Joint Committee–Toronto Island Airport was struck. That year eight government bodies began the creation of eight different studies on the Toronto Island Airport. In 1977, the voluminous "Access Alternatives" was released. With mind-boggling cross-referencing, it detailed all the alternative ways of getting to the island depending on what happened to the airport itself and if marine parks, housing developments, and other proposals for island land became reality.

Costs, revenues, reliability, and the impact on the environment, on marine traffic, on the mainland, and on congestion were all factored in.

The conclusion? There wasn't one. Just alternatives.

And so, by 1982, nothing had changed. Another good study came out, though. This report came tantalizingly close to a whole new approach, a platform rig that would rest on rails on the bottom of the lake. "This type of facility would not be affected by wave action created by bad weather conditions nor would it interfere with other marine traffic on the gap," the report suggested.

But the study group couldn't find any data on building a rig, so the idea was dropped.

And so the eighties came and went with more proposals for ways to get to the island. Consultants even studied the idea of spending $20 million to fill the channel in and create a new one south of the airport.

In 1989 no less than a Royal Commission studied the Western Gap. Because of recent political agreements that prohibited a vehicular tunnel or bridge and the exorbitant costs of a pedestrian tunnel, nothing could be done, the commission concluded.

In the nineties several more attempts were made to build a fixed link.

Perhaps, somebody reasoned, what was needed was a committee with a really long name, a name that would inspire trust and investment and hint at the kind of length required to fill a hundred-metre gap.

The Intergovernmental Staff Committee Study of Alternative Access Options to the Island Airport for Emergency Response Services triumphantly concluded in March of 1993 that a movable bridge was best.

It's not clear what happened next, but the best guess is that the committee's effort sank under the weight of its own name.

The Toronto Harbour Commission, which operated the Toronto City Centre Airport, tried again in 1996, this time with the backing of the city. Its report examined the problems of relying on ferries — moving emergency vehicles to the airport, delays because of mechanical failures, and the fact that they don't operate at night. And the ferry service was still operating at a loss, about $1.1 million in 1992.

The best idea was a lift bridge at the end of Bathurst Street that "should be conceived as an important civic monument," a "pleasant pedestrian destination offering unique views of the city and the harbour."

A consultant's report based on that consultant's report wholeheartedly agreed.

A moveable bridge of some kind, one that either lifted or swung, or maybe a bascule bridge, costing $10 million, would work well, especially if commercial traffic found another way to Toronto Harbour.

No bascule, lift, or swing bridge went up.

The new millennium came and brought new reports that differed largely from the old reports by the fact the dates now read 2000-something instead of 1900-something.

There were also some catchier titles for the reports. "Our Toronto Waterfront: Gateway to the New Canada" was the public pitch put on top of the official Toronto Waterfront Revitalization Task Force report. There was also the Community Airport Impact Review, or Community AIR (get it?). As usual, once everyone cast their eyes to the waterfront, they then cast their eyes to the airport — resulting in several new assessments — and then to the gap.

Finally, in 2002, Toronto City Council approved a bridge to the island. Polls showed more than half of Torontonians opposed building a bridge. People in Toronto like having their own island. It's a much more peaceful place than the city. In the 2003 municipal election race, David Miller ran for mayor on a fixed platform, so to speak, of opposing a bridge. He won and immediately killed the idea. After a series of threatened lawsuits, the federal government paid the Toronto Airport Authority $35 million for the cancellation of the project. That's fine, Miller says, now Toronto can get $27 million in back taxes from the authority.

And so it went, much as it had in the past, with no end and no fixed link in sight.

CHAPTER 5

WAR

To heck with being peacekeepers. We Canadians like to mix it up sometimes. The world's our hockey game, damn it. Now and then, we're just a little offside.

You give us furs and we'll give you, let's see, bitter enemies

Samuel de Champlain was certainly a great explorer. And as far as Europeans went, he was progressive in his ideas about natives — well, at least the good Canadian natives. But as an ally, he could be pretty dangerous.

When Champlain and other French explorers and traders came over to the New World they hooked up with the Hurons, the great nation of about thirty thousand people stretched across present-day Ontario. The Hurons held a key piece of territory located between the fur-trading Algonquin tribes to the north and the agricultural Petuns and Neutrals in the south. They traded and got along with both, and when the French arrived the Hurons became the most important link to the valuable fur trade. In return for pelts, the Hurons got steel knives and copper kettles and other European-made goods that made life a lot easier.

That didn't sit too well with their traditional rivals, the Iroquois, who lived further south. Although they came from the same origins, the Hurons and Iroquois had become bitter enemies.

Over the years, historians have labelled one tribe or the other as the good guys, depending on whatever suited their purpose. After the Civil War, a U.S. historian determined the Iroquois were the good guys because they had a strong central government, much like the victorious North. The Hurons were a lot like the South, a loose confederation of tribes. A Canadian historian turned the tables on that theory a hundred years later during the Cold War, viewing the peace-loving Hurons as akin to the West, and the war-like, nationalistic Iroquois as akin to the Soviet Union.

Looking back, the only thing we know for sure is that as soon as Europeans meddled, disaster followed.

As the Dutch traders in colonies to the south and the French in colonies to the north competed for the fur trade, so did their respective allies, the Iroquois and the Hurons. By 1615, Iroquois raiding parties were pestering the Hurons so much that they were having trouble delivering their furs to the French. The Hurons asked Champlain for help. Champlain agreed, because in return he would finally get to explore the Huron territory and break the trail for others to convert the Hurons to Christianity. Champlain and two other Frenchmen, accompanied by ten natives, travelled deep into Huron country, around present-day Orillia, Ontario, in the summer of 1615. Then a war party canoed down to Lake Ontario and across the water into Iroquois land. They snuck up to an Iroquois stronghold near Lake Onondaga and prepared to attack.

Champlain wasn't too happy with what he saw before him, a fortified village with thirty-foot-high palisades and a ready supply of water in a nearby pond. That high up, the Iroquois could rain arrows down on any invaders. No matter — a well-organized force and a twelve-foot tower from which to shoot into the fort would teach those Iroquois a lesson. The French and Hurons built the tower and a mantelet, a large, moveable shelter to shield fighters from the arrows raining down from the fort.

Things didn't quite work out as planned. The Hurons weren't used to organized fighting and kept breaking ranks. The battle ended in a stalemate, with Champlain himself suffering two arrow wounds. Reinforcements from another Huron village never arrived, so the French and Huron warriors gave up and returned home.

The Iroquois couldn't help but notice the French helping out their rivals in an attack on Iroquois territory. That did not make the Iroquois happy, and upsetting the Iroquois was like upsetting a nest of bees. The Iroquois shouted at Champlain during the battle to mind his own business.

That Champlain did not do. In fact, he spent the winter with the Hurons, cementing the alliance between the French and the native nation. That in turn led to Jesuits pouring into the Huron nation to convert the natives.

The Iroquois, meanwhile, grew even angrier at the French and the Hurons, who now had a stranglehold on the fur trade. The fur trade brought European weapons and goods to the Hurons, and that didn't sit well with the Iroquois. The Hurons and Iroquois made attempts to make peace, but the French broke up any efforts. They were afraid that an alliance of Hurons and Iroquois might help the French rivals, the Dutch, to seize the fur trade.

That was just too much for the Iroquois. They began invading Huron territory in earnest. At about the same time, thanks to the French, smallpox raged through the Huron territory, killing about eighteen thousand of the thirty-thousand-strong nation in 1637 alone. The Iroquois methodically destroyed the Neutrals and Petuns, the Huron allies to the south, and then went after the Hurons themselves in 1648 and 1649. A thousand Iroquois warriors slipped into Huron territory over the winter of 1648–49, unnoticed by any scouts, and began a series of surprise attacks on Huron villages in March 1649.

Over the summer, the terrified Hurons and Jesuits fled to an island in Georgian Bay, now called Christian Island. It turned out to be no refuge. Only eight thousand Hurons were left, but the island wasn't big enough to support even that reduced number. Over the winter of 1649–50, four thousand more Hurons died of famine, disease, and exposure. The Iroquois spent the winter picking off anybody who tried to make it off the island and had a field day in the spring when survivors tried en masse to escape their self-imposed island prison. Some of them did make it safely into Quebec or into friendly Ojibway territory to the north.

Of the thirty thousand Hurons thriving when Champlain arrived, only three hundred of his allies were left by 1650.

It's no surprise that today, the statue of Champlain standing tall over his Huron friends in a park in Orillia isn't all that popular with a nearby Ojibway community.

Thanks for the fort, now give us the rest of the state

Once upon a time, the United States was terrified of being attacked, so it put security on its northern border on high alert. No, this is not a post-9/11 story. This is a post-1812 story.

In fact they were so terrified of an attack on their northern border that they started building a fort on the northern tip of Lake Champlain at Sand Island near Rouses Point in 1816.

There was a good reason for putting the fort there. It was on a route Americans liked to take when they were attacking Canada, so it wouldn't hurt to make sure it wasn't used in reverse. (And other armies had recognized its value. French commanders had attacked the British through this route during the Seven Years War and the British marched down after the Americans had marched up it during the War of 1812.)

There was one good reason for *not* putting the fort there. The fort was actually in Canada. The Americans had worked for three years building the fort when military leaders realized their mistake and abandoned it. The locals felt entitled to help themselves to parts of the fort for use in their own buildings.

Thirty years later a treaty between the two countries moved the border slightly north, placing the fort back in the U.S. Still fearing an attack from the north, the Americans started building a second fort on the same site. Fort Montgomery was named after General Dick Montgomery, who had led the army up that route in the late 1700s, heading north with the plan to liberate Quebec. As it turned out, the Quebecois declined the offer and chased the Yanks back through the bush in the middle of winter.

Nonetheless, Fort Montgomery was a fine piece of military engineering and cutting-edge technology for the times. No fewer than five masonry walls surrounded the core and mighty gates and bastions were added. Lots of gunnery was put in place, including seventy cannon.

As it turned out, the real threat to the United States was from within. In the middle of the 1800s, the war that was to wind up killing more Americans than any other erupted when the northern states and southern states declared war on each other.

The American Civil War did much to hone arms manufacturers' skills around the world, and with the advances made in guns, masonry forts could be smashed to gravel. So by the time the second version of Fort Montgomery was finished, it was obsolete.

And — like its predecessor — it was ransacked by locals and used for local buildings. The final insult to the fort took place during the Great Depression, when the Works Project Administration hired locals to pull down the masonry walls and crush them into gravel to be used in the construction of a bridge from Rouses Point across to Alberg, which looks down on the ruins of the fort better known by its nickname: Fort Blunder.

Pick a side, any side

Occasional Canadian Joseph Willcocks never could decide what side he was on, until a battle decided for him.

Born into an upper-class British family in Ireland, Willcocks arrived in Upper Canada in 1799 and first latched onto the powerful elite of Upper Canada in the early 1800s. With the help of influential friends, he served for a while as the sheriff of York and as an assistant to a couple of judges.

Despite his ties to the elite, he soon turned on it, establishing a newspaper called the *Upper Canadian Guardian; or, Freeman's Journal*, based out of Newark in the Niagara region. Through the newspaper he viciously attacked the administration running Upper Canada. That elite certainly deserved a shake-up, and Willcocks's views got him elected to the Lower Assembly (Upper Canada had both an upper and lower legislative assembly then). But Willcocks, who was in the habit of going too far, was twice jailed for criminal libel.

At the beginning of the War of 1812, Willcocks successfully fought against Isaac Brock's attempt to invoke martial law. Then he suddenly joined Brock and agreed to persuade the natives living on the Grand River to join the British cause. He even fought beside Brock at Queenston Heights, where the general was killed.

Then, a year later, while still a member of the Assembly, he decided the Americans were the right side in the war and were probably going to win. So he started passing on secrets about British troop movements to the U.S. Secretary of War.

Even that wasn't good enough for Willcocks. He then joined the U.S. army as colonel while still serving as a member of the Upper Canada Lower Assembly. The Assembly kicked him out.

You'd think Willcocks would have been a merciful commander, given he was fighting against his old country. Not quite. He used his command of about one hundred troops in slash-and-burn expeditions that often targeted his old political enemies. Despite his professed belief in helping ordinary people, he had no problem burning their houses and barns and turning women and children into the street, regardless of the season. He particularly enjoyed leading the burning of his old hometown, Newark.

Willcocks eluded several attempts to capture him. He finally died as an American in the siege of Fort Erie in 1814.

Well, it was good exercise

The Fenians are coming! The Fenians are coming!

Nothing roused the border towns and cities of Canada in the mid-1800s like the call of an invasion from the secret Irish-American Fenian brotherhood.

And nowhere was the answer to that call of invasion more stirring than in Manitoba in 1871.

"Rally then at once!" commanded the official proclamation from Governor George Archibald. "We rely upon the prompt response of all our people of every origin to this, Our call."

Nowhere did greater heroes answer the call than in Manitoba. Brush aside the fact few involved actually met, saw, attacked, or captured the dread Fenian. The intent of heroism was real. And so were the dangers. Indeed, one soldier even fell in the mud.

The Fenian threat was real elsewhere in Canada. Organized in New York in 1859, the Fenian brotherhood was committed to liberating Ireland from Britain. That didn't work out so well. When former Civil War soldiers swelled the ranks six years later, however, the Fenians turned their eyes north. A successful invasion of the country that was formerly a British colony would liberate fellow Irishmen and provide a base of operations. The Fenians did more than just talk about attacking. Two hundred of them invaded Canada near Fort Erie on June 2, 1867, and were driven back. Another eighteen hundred poured into the Eastern Townships of Quebec two days later and plundered several towns before retreating. So when word came in September 1871 that two thousand Fenians were massed along the Manitoba border, it was easy to believe that the province was in danger.

The Honourable Gilbert McMicken, newly appointed Agent of the Dominion Lands for Manitoba, rushed from Windsor, Ontario, to the neighbouring and threatened province. He told his story seventeen years later to the Historical and Scientific Society of Manitoba and pulled no punches about his own key role.

On his way to Fort Garry (a Hudson's Bay Company fort near present-day Winnipeg) through the United States, he gathered intelligence about the threat, which suddenly involved the prospect of rebellion by the Metis.

"I was full impressed ... that, however insignificant the Fenian force might be, there was great and immediate danger of general rising of the French Half Breeds and was burning with impatience to reach Fort Garry," McMicken recounted.

Library and Archives Canada/PA-051598

Sometime after he rallied Manitoba to fend off an invasion that never happened, Gilbert McMicken, Dominion Lands agent for the area, posed for a photograph outside Fort Garry with the secretary to Lt.-Gov. Norris and a pony.

He even interviewed an innkeeper's wife about conversations she had overheard earlier that week concerning a rebellion. McMicken was convinced of the deadly possibility of widespread rebellion and large-scale invasion. (He was later publicly ridiculed for using the story of an innkeeper's wife as a key piece of intelligence. The Metis did not rise up and rebel because of a Fenian invasion. In fact, they offered to help fight.)

Worried as he was, McMicken let nothing imperil his journey to Fort Garry, not the raging prairie fires, a reluctant stagecoach driver —

"vile … lame lump of humanity" — or warnings that he was prey to Fenian supporters and robbers.

"You will be robbed and killed to a certainty," he was warned.

"Danger could not sway me from a conviction of the necessity of doing all in my power to accomplish the performance of the duty I was charged with," McMicken vowed.

Once in Fort Garry, on Monday, October 2, it was he who convinced Lieutenant-Governor Archibald to raise the alarm.

Archibald's proclamation the next day went straight to the heart of the Fenian threat: "They intend to make a raid into this Province from a country with which we are at peace and to commit acts of depredation, pillage and other outrages upon the persons and property of our loving subjects. While not unprepared to meet the emergency without regular forces, We do hereby warn all Our said loving subjects to put themselves in readiness at once to assist in repelling this outrage upon their hearths and homes."

The response was overwhelming. "No proclamation ever met with a more hearty response," reported the *Manitoban*. "Two hours after the proclamation was issued, the men of Winnipeg turned out almost to a man and a monster meeting was held at the Court Room."

The courtroom was so crowded that men were forced to gather outside. After "stirring speeches" and "addresses replete with force and power," the men signed up to fight back the Fenian hordes.

More than one hundred men signed up, including sixty from the Hudson's Bay Company. The next day forty men from Mapleton marched thirty miles to Winnipeg to join up, followed the day after by dozens from the nearby Parish of Kildonan.

Then they waited. The stage from the border town of Pembina came Wednesday, with no passengers and no word. "The driver could give no more information than his horses," the *Manitoban* reported.

Thursday came and went, still with no information. Finally, on Friday, October 6, Fort Garry learned the Fenians had crossed the border at Pembina and sacked the Hudson's Bay post. They were on their way to Fort Garry.

Military leaders quickly organized the militia under various companies. So eager was everyone to beat back the Fenians that those ordered to stay behind and guard the fort begged to go with the rest.

"At half past two o'clock on Friday afternoon, Fort Garry presented a lively aspect. It was wet and cold and muddy and everything tended to dampen the general enthusiasm, but though nature did her utmost in this respect it was of no avail," the *Manitoban* reported.

It took all afternoon to gather the forces.

"It began to approach to darkness and the rain fell, and it was terrible busy and the commissariat and Major Peebles were busy, and then the bugle sounded."

Three companies of infantry and an artillery company, about two hundred men, marched out of the fort. Then they waited some more. There was only one old scow available to ferry the entire force across the Assiniboine River, forcing soldiers to wait on the south shore in the cold, wet darkness for hours.

The crossing itself was dramatic. One of the Winnipeg Home Guards was helping on the scow when he fell into the river, sank in the mud, and had to be pulled out. Major Peebles came close to death when he urged his horse off the scow and onto the landing. One of the horse's back hooves missed the landing and horse and rider fell back into the muddy river. The officer was rescued immediately, but it took about forty-five minutes to get the horse out of the mud. After struggling to pull him out, soldiers took another look at the situation. Someone took his rifle and, by poking its rump with the point of a bayonet, urged the horse out.

Then the troops had to march through the dark and deep mud to St. Norbert. The dangers were many, especially from each other.

As the soldiers marched in close quarters, their rifles slung backwards on their shoulders, "the muzzle of the rifle of a man in front punched one in the face, while the butt of the rifle from behind banged the unfortunate on the back of the head," recalled one veteran, C.N. Belle. He was a member of the artillery, transporting a brass cannon to the front. The cannon, he reported, kept getting overturned in the mud.

The mounted troops faced their own dangers. At least one, a Hudson's Bay factor, fell off his horse and, reported McMickin, "an intimate acquaintance was made with the prairie."

The troops marched for two days in the muck and rain, reaching St. Agathe on the Sunday.

There they learned the sad truth.

On the day before they left Fort Garry, Thursday, October 5, U.S. Colonel Lloyd Wheaton had come across the Fenians looting the Hudson's Bay post at Pembina and arrested the leaders and half of the twenty-strong force.

"I think further anxiety regarding a Fenian invasion of Manitoba unnecessary," Colonel Wheaten wrote in a dispatch to the U.S. consul in Winnipeg.

The tired troops from Fort Garry had to turn around and march two days back home, with nothing to show for their troubles but bruised heads.

After all this, they expect us to fight?

It was a scary time for Canadians in the late 1800s. The country had made its way past a minor rebellion in the 1830s and blundered through the Fenian raids in the 1860s, a comedy of errors that sometimes turned bloody. But in 1885, the first real military test came. For some troops, the first test was actually making it to the battlefront.

Less than twenty years had passed since Confederation. On March 27, 1885, the orders came to mobilize the militia in Ontario to put down a rebellion in Manitoba. The Grey and Simcoe Foresters were included in that mobilization order. This included troops from across central and northern Simcoe County.

The trick was getting the troops to Manitoba.

Whether this figured in the strategies of Louis Riel is not known. But certainly one of the challenges facing the men heading west that early spring was how they would actually get to the battle.

They couldn't march out. There was still snow in Simcoe County in early spring; in the north, the winter would last even longer.

They might have taken ships through the Great Lakes to the end of Lake Superior, then headed by train through the United States to St. Paul, Minnesota. From there they could march to Fort Garry, now part of Winnipeg.

But according to Brian A. Brown in his book *Foresters: The Canadian Quest for Peace*, a trip through the U.S. would have meant a certain amount of humiliation — and a potential for lost luggage.

"The trouble with travelling through the United States was that the militia would have to be disarmed and travel in civilian clothing as private citizens with their munitions, rifles and artillery boxed for shipment in the baggage cars. Public transportation was no more reliable than it is now with respect to guaranteed delivery of baggage."

The Canadian railway was not yet complete. While it spanned the West, the rocky outcrops, rivers, lakes, swamps, and forests of Northern Ontario had slowed the progress of the rail ribbon that would eventually tie the country together.

Nonetheless, William Cornelius Van Horne, the president of Canadian Pacific, wanted to prove the value of his railway by having the troops move west on it. Sure, the railway wasn't complete, but Van Horne promised to have the first troops in Fort Garry within ten days. The entire force of more than 3,300 men would be west within a fortnight.

And they were — once they actually left.

The order for mobilization came on a Friday. Then it took a day for the officers to get word out to the area farms and through the sawmill villages and towns. At ten o'clock on Saturday morning, the troops were mustered. In Barrie, two hundred men, some, according to Brown, carrying supplies, were ready to leave immediately. Instead, they were updated on the situation, drilled, and sent home with orders to muster again on Monday.

On the day after April Fool's Day, spirits were high among the men on the train that pulled out of Barrie. In order to go west they had to travel east to Smith's Falls, near Ottawa, then northwest to North Bay, Sudbury, and onward.

It was shortly after midnight when they reached the first break in the rail line, at Dog Lake. The temperature, according to records, was around freezing, but according to Brown, the reception was warm, with lots of food.

After dinner, the troops were organized into formation and mounted a long line of horse-drawn sleighs that would carry them to the next rail link before the morning sun turned the frozen snow into impassable mush.

"The sleighs were intended for eight men, but there were frequently 10 or 12 jammed in. There were frequent sections where the roadbed was not yet constructed or where the bridges remained to be built, in which case, the sleighs would have to follow the tote road, often for many miles through forests, over stumps and rocks, on and on for hour after hour," said Brown.

As the troops bumped over the rough track in the frozen darkness, at times being dumped into the snow or freezing sloughs of slush, the high spirits began to wane. War wasn't so glamorous.

They arrived at Magpie a few hours before dawn. This small camp — and the promise of rest — must have seemed like heaven. But as the exhausted, frostbitten men made their way to the bunkhouses, the bugle blew for breakfast.

The doors opened to the bunkhouses, showing makeshift kitchens where beds should have been. Pork and beans were served, and farm boys and shop clerks sat down in the snow to eat. It was twenty below freezing when they arrived. By the time they finished their breakfast, it had warmed enough to snow.

Once they'd finished, the order was given to remount the sleighs to finish this leg of the journey — another four hours. In all, the trip was forty miles. For the last few hours, the temperature continued to rise, turning the snow into sleet, which coated the men, sleighs, horses, and equipment.

They arrived at the next camp, cheerily called Desolation, at 8:30 a.m. on April 5, wet, cold, and miserable. Some of the men had collapsed with exhaustion on the sleighs. Most of the men ignored the cook tent and crammed themselves into the few beds available. At 11:00 a.m. they were awakened to board the train.

The train was a collection of utility cars — not a passenger or dining car among them. Some were open gravel cars and others had a roof but only slats for sides.

The train left the tracks, falling over into the snow, twice on the way to the next stop. The top speed of the train was five miles per hour. Three hours later, the train pulled into Bandeville. The men were fed sandwiches and hot drinks. After a brief rest, they piled back onto the train and headed onwards to Port Munro. At 11:00 p.m., some twelve hours after leaving Desolation, they arrived at the port, where there was a bed for every man.

Many men slept past breakfast, lunch, and dinner, waking only to clamber back on the sleighs in the night. The trip would be across the frozen waters of Lake Superior; to cross during the day would mean dealing with slush and with snow blindness.

As the small army set out, the wind kicked up, blowing freshly fall-en snow into whiteouts. The whiteouts gave way to broken landscapes of hard ice and then glare ice. The miracle was that no one fell by the way-side or was frozen to death.

At 2:00 a.m., they trooped into McKellar's Harbour, their limbs frozen stiff in their pants and jackets. A train waited for them, with more open cars. The men, beyond caring, piled on.

They travelled another fifteen miles to Jackfish Bay and breakfast and bunks.

The next day, they assembled in formation and split into two groups, both heading off on sleighs. The sleighs for the second group forced the laden sleighs of the first group off the trail, where many men were thrown out of overturned sleighs — again.

It took six hours for the first group to reach Winston's Dock. The second group arrived at midnight, and they all loaded onto another train and headed to Nipigon, at that time a small village.

They were promised it was only a ten-mile march to the final section of track that would take them to Fort Garry in a single day. But it was ten miles through a trail that had once been covered in four feet of snow and was now slush.

Part of the journey was over lake ice, which was also now slush. The temperature had warmed considerably but that didn't help — it was now thundering and raining.

They arrived in Red Rock at 3:00 a.m. on April 9 and once again boarded trains. But this time, the exhausted men dropped into plush seats in the best cars of the entire journey.

Not one life was lost during the trip. But already, the men had expe-rienced more misery than they had their entire lives. And the first shot had yet to be fired.

My police officer can beat up your police officer

It was just another day in Rat Portage, Manitoba, er ... Rat Portage, Ontario.

Manitoba police in town charged shopkeeper Malcolm McQuarrie with selling liquor without a licence.

But I have a licence, McQuarrie argued.

Not from Manitoba, came the response. Yours is from Ontario.

When Ontario police, also in the same town, heard about the charge, they stationed a squad of men by the store to prevent McQuarrie's arrest.

Manitoba's attorney general himself came to Rat Portage and insisted on McQuarrie's arrest. When four Manitoba officers, including the Manitoba police chief, entered the store to arrest McQuarrie, the Ontario police officers arrested the Manitoba chief.

In the confusion, the other three Manitoba officers started hauling McQuarrie away.

Then they were arrested by a group of Ontario officers and locked in jail.

There was nothing unusual about this incident on November 23, 1883.

All of those charged, themselves charging others, could look forward to appearing before a Manitoba magistrate or an Ontario magistrate. Unless, of course, as happened now and then, police from the opposing province arrested the magistrate.

Such was life in the split personality town of Rat Portage in the 1880s, an example of perhaps the most comical failure of political and police jurisdiction in Canada.

Ontario preceded Manitoba into Confederation by three years, but the vast area north of the Great Lakes was anybody's at the time.

Soon after joining Confederation in 1870, Manitoba claimed a much larger territory north of what was then a tiny province. Ontario also started making claims on the land. As federal governments rose and fell, different acts of Parliament gave both Manitoba and Ontario jurisdiction over the area.

The mess appeared to be cleared up in 1881, when the federal government proclaimed an act to extend the boundaries of Manitoba.

Unfortunately, yet typical of the federal government, the act didn't exactly state where those boundaries would sit.

Even so, Manitoba jumped at the chance to govern the area and appointed constables, a coroner, and other public officials and set up a court and jail in Rat Portage. Aside from a few speeches from politicians, Ontario didn't do much until Manitoba announced it was holding provincial elections in 1883. Rat Portage would be part of those elections.

That woke Ontario up. It sent six constables to Rat Portage, built a jail, appointed a magistrate, and started issuing liquor licences. Those liquor licences turned into the key battleground for the Rat Portage war.

Ontario police arrested shopkeepers selling liquor under Manitoba licences. Manitoba police arrested shopkeepers selling liquor under Ontario licences. Then Ontario police arrested Manitoba police for arresting people with Ontario licences and Manitoba police arrested Ontario police for arresting people with Manitoba licences. Prisoners being escorted to jail were often freed by parties representing one province or another.

In one incident, two Ontario constables arrested for selling liquor were convicted and sent to jail. Ontario supporters set fire to the stables behind a hotel owned by a Manitoba justice to get police away from the Manitoba jail and used the diversion to free the Ontario constables. Manitoba constables arrested several suspects for the arson but were stopped on the way to the Manitoba jail and themselves thrown in the Ontario jail by the Ontario constables.

Meanwhile, the Ontario magistrate ordered the arrest of the Manitoba magistrate and Manitoba constables who had put the two Ontario constables in jail in the first place. None too happy about this, the rest of the Manitoba constables threw everyone they could find using an Ontario liquor licence in jail. The next day a mob of 150 people battered down the door of the jail, freed the Ontario prisoners, and burnt the jail down.

Because things were going so swimmingly well, the Ontario government then announced it too was holding elections on September 28.

Although emotions ran high before the election, with Manitoba sending in soldiers, the elections went ahead. Rat Portage now had two of everything, from municipal clerks on up to members of provincial parliament. Lucky Rat Portage.

A few more years, and I'll know everything about their pubs

During the Second World War, the German navy and secret service planned and performed several missions and offensive operations along the Canadian coast. While our military worked bravely to defend us, in some cases they didn't have to do much to keep us safe.

One of these missions began in May 1942 when the German submarine U-213 slipped undetected into the Bay of Fundy with a "Lieutenant Langbein" aboard. He was a spy who was equipped with a false Canadian identity, a portable transmitter-receiver, civilian clothes, and a substantial amount of money.

He landed on the shore at Melvin's Beach, east of St. Martins, and made his way to some cover at the edge of the beach, as the crew paddled back to the submarine in their inflatable raft. With U-213 disappearing into the salty water of Fundy in a froth of bubbles, Langbein, as instructed, dug a hole in the sand and buried his naval uniform and his radio. Then he started his nefarious work. Well, sort of.

Langbein walked the two and a half hours to St. Martins and eventually made his way to Saint John, Moncton, and Montreal, finally reaching Ottawa. He remained undetected for more than two years — perhaps not all that surprising considering that he didn't actually perform any espionage. Apparently he considered himself not so much a spy as, say, a tourist.

Finally, in December 1944, having run out of the money given to him by Germany to finance his espionage activities, he turned himself in to the Canadian authorities. He was tried but acquitted — the jury stated he had not committed any hostile act against Canada.

Two months after the election, when shopkeeper McQuarrie's arrest led to simultaneous arrests of just about everyone, Ontario's and Manitoba's provincial leaders came to their senses and agreed to let the Queen's Privy Council decide which province owned the town. On August 11, 1884, the council gave the land to Ontario.

Rat Portage, an unattractive name that was bound to inspire trouble in the first place, became Kenora. The bitterness passed. Regular Manitoba and Ontario folk got along just fine. They all learned one valuable lesson. The more government a town has, the more poorly it is governed.

War is no picnic, especially if the sandwiches are stale

A lovely time was had by all.

In Innisfail, Alberta, visitors enjoyed a plate of stew, biscuits, and plum pudding. In Strathmore, Alberta, people partook of ten-cent bingo sponsored by the Lions Club. In Crossfield, Alberta, "many families had brought their own lunch and a cheerful atmosphere prevailed as they chatted among themselves and their neighbours."

The nearby town of Airdrie outdid itself. "Members of the Ladies Community Club operated a lunch counter and coffee, tea and sandwiches for five cents were available. … After lunch, the children hurried upstairs to see the free movie provided for them and the Hollywood musical kept the youngsters entertained for nearly two hours," reported the *Calgary Herald*. Said one seven-year-old girl to friends, "Gee, we had a swell time and saw a free movie."

Ah, the innocence of youth. The enduring nature of the human spirit. All cheerfulness and pleasantries aside, the hundreds of visitors arriving in small towns around Calgary that September day in 1955 were the foundation of an exercise that the *Herald* proclaimed held up nothing less than "THE SURVIVAL ON THIS EARTH OF THE HUMAN SPECIES."

"The public has never been told the stark truth, bluntly, as it was told to me by an internationally respected authority … there is one basic

In the civil defence control centre at the Royal Canadian Air Force airport, leaders of the exercise plotted the progress of Operation Lifesaver and reported to headquarters using Boy Scouts as runners.

thing that occupies the minds of the leaders of the Western world … THE SURVIVAL ON THIS EARTH OF THE HUMAN SPECIES. And the hope is: THAT THERE WILL BE SUFFICIENT PEOPLE LEFT ALIVE AND HEALTHY TO BREED AND PRESERVE THE SPECIES."

The best way to do that, figured Calgary's civil defence leader Geoffrey Bell, was to move everyone out of the city.

Most civil defence leaders of the day thought the best plan was to construct a fallout shelter and hide. Bell would have nothing to do with that. A retired British army officer, Bell had no trouble convincing Calgary Mayor Don Mackay that the city must run an evacuation test.

On February 11, 1955, Mayor Mackay, Provincial Secretary-Treasurer C.E. Gerhart, and National Health and Welfare Minister Paul Martin announced plans for a mass civil defence evacuation exercise, the largest of its kind in Canada. About forty thousand Calgarians were to be moved out of the city and into nearby towns. The scale of the plan was unprecedented, and it attracted international attention. NATO decided to send observers. Calgarians grew even prouder to learn that Vancouver officials had also been considered for the plan but backed out. The fools.

Over the summer, civil defence and military authorities worked on the plan. They came up with a bold title, Operation Lifesaver, and a bold plan, moving forty thousand Calgarians in the northeast section of the city to seventeen small communities north and northeast of the city.

The date was set: Wednesday, September 21, 1955.

All the proper preparations were put in place.

Bell and other civil defence leaders would direct the exercise in a bombproof bunker built at the municipal golf course at a cost of $70,000. They were equipped with two-way radios and telephones.

The drill hall at RCAF Station Calgary was turned into a war room, with large communications boards, a scale map of the evacuation area, and a meteorological board. Besides military personnel and civil defence observers, there were switchboard operators, clerks, and four Boy Scouts on hand to provide support. The Boy Scouts were to transmit messages coming in from shortwave radio and telephone.

The northeast part of the city was divided into twenty-one zones of civil defence. Pamphlets outlining the evacuation were delivered to each home in the area. Residents of each zone were to go to a specific town when the evacuation siren sounded. Each family was to pack food and clothing for twenty-four hours and follow colour-coded road signs to their destination. Those without their own cars were to go to one of sixteen assembly areas to catch a ride with volunteer drivers and car owners. Transit service in downtown Calgary would be shut down for two hours. Even insurance coverage was arranged for participants who might get in a car accident or sustain property damage during the exercise.

In the seventeen designated towns north of Calgary, volunteers made sandwiches, got bingo cards ready, and set up projectors for the city folk who would spend hours in their community halls.

Sometime after 10:00 a.m. on Wednesday, September 21 — the exact time was a surprise to better replicate a real evacuation — the sirens would wail. The evacuees would stay until an all-clear signal was given and transmitted by phone or radio to the towns. Meanwhile, the evacuated neighbourhoods would be closed to all but emergency traffic and patrolled by police to stop would-be vandals and looters.

On the eve of the test, all was ready.

"I am perfectly satisfied with our plans and we've been told by others who have studied it that it is sound," announced Bell the day before the test.

Then it snowed. And rained. And the wind blew. And the temperature dropped from 25°C to about 3°C.

Five inches of snow fell from noon Tuesday to Wednesday morning. The highways leading out of Calgary, some of them hazardous at the best of times, were passable but slippery. The smaller roads leading to the seventeen towns and the roads in the towns themselves became quagmires. A mobile civil defence unit got stuck near Langdon Corner.

At 9:30 a.m., Operation Lifesaver was postponed. It was simply too dangerous to drive. Especially, the mayor noted at the time, because many of the men of the households had to keep working that day and the cars were to be driven by "the ladies of the home."

The good news? It was unlikely that an attack would occur in such terrible conditions anyway.

In the seventeen towns set to receive the city folk, volunteers put their thousands of sandwiches in cold storage.

In Three Hills, however, the three hundred loaves of bread made into sandwiches would not last, officials determined. Three Hills would not pull out of the plan but decided instead that next time only coffee and doughnuts would be served. There is no report on the reaction of Calgarians living in Civil Defence Zone 7, who would be heading to Three Hills and not a sandwich-laden town during the next exercise.

Over the next week, the civil defenders kept up a brave front. Most of the civil defence observers from elsewhere in Canada and the United States, including Major-General Penhale from the civil defence college in Arnprior, left, with no plans to return. Civil defence authorities chose Wednesday, September 28, as the new date for the test.

Critics of the plan, and there were a few, raised their own alarm. A Calgary alderman named P.N.R. Morrison accused civil defence director Bell of "rank incompetence." Choosing the fall for the removal of forty thousand people was simply daft, considering the volatile weather of autumn in Calgary, Morrison said. He claimed that he asked the civil defence directors three months ago what would happen if weather conditions were poor and got no answer.

The idea itself was flawed, Morrison continued. The evacuation of a city would rely not on a "huge publicity stunt" but on educating residents what to do in case of a disaster or attack.

"It requires no 90-mile trek into the country to play bingo to demonstrate that Calgarians can drive in convoy. They prove that between here and Banff every Sunday during the summer," Morrison said.

"September 21 has come and gone and found Calgary with a civil defence which could not save one single life because we had a storm … Other cities, instead of planning massive convoy groupings to accommodate enemy marksmen, are planning survival within the city and in the scattered populations around it."

Bell admitted Morrison had asked about the weather but added weather records showed that in eight of the past ten years, September 21 had "beautiful weather." The *Calgary Herald* took Morrison to task, calling his "coldly calculated attempt to wreck Operation Lifesaver … thoroughly ill-considered and totally irresponsible." The best military minds in the world can think of nothing better than mass evacuations in times of war, the *Herald* stated.

The *Herald* then pulled out all the stops to persuade people to participate. A front-page column by a reporter who had witnessed the devastation of Pearl Harbor warned Calgarians that they were not invulnerable from an attack. The *Herald* editorial the day before the exercise proclaimed it "the plain duty of every responsible citizen to co-operate as fully as possible."

Plain duty or not, an informal poll taken the day before the September 28 exercise showed half of fifty families would participate, on one condition. "If the weather is nice," said Patrick Gordon, "we'll go." Other people who had booked off September 21 for the first exercise were unable to get another day off.

The day of the second evacuation attempt dawned with a cool light rain. At 10:50 a.m., September 28, 1955, air raid sirens sounded. Many people didn't hear them or didn't understand them. Most residents expected sirens to make the long wailing sound familiar to people during the Second World War, but the federal government had changed the sound to a series of short blasts. Those who didn't understand the sirens, though, listened to their radios or got word over the phone. Around 1:00 p.m. smoke bombs went off in northeast Calgary. "Enemy bombers" flew in from the north.

"Formation late four engine, unidentified bombers, presumed hostile, sighted headed towards Calgary. These aircraft may be expected arrive Calgary 1:30 p.m.," the Alberta civil defence bulletin read.

No one really explained why Calgary, an inland city, was chosen as the target of enemy hordes or how the planes managed to get overland without being shot down by, say, a farmer with a good rifle.

Hundreds of northeast Calgarians did not worry about those minor details. They got in their cars and headed north. Some Calgarians were eager to join in, so eager that they lined up at assembly areas for rides out of the city before the sirens even sounded. No Commie was going to catch Calgary sleeping in.

The *Herald* blanketed the region with reporters. In fact, 126 journalists from across Canada, including a National Film Board crew, covered the evacuation.

There were the usual war stories of loss and redemption. Some cars got stuck in the mud and other drivers helped them out. Battles were also bravely fought behind the scenes. Dr. A.J. Keys, medical officer of health for the Municipal District of Wheatland No. 40, took on the awesome responsibility of inspecting the sandwiches put into deep freeze in Strathmore the week before. With the skills only a medical man can offer and the resoluteness of a born leader, he checked those sandwiches and declared them fit for consumption. The coffee had to be brewed fresh.

"War," intoned Mayor D.H. Mackay in his address to the public that morning, "is not a Sunday afternoon picnic experience."

The next day, Operation Lifesaver officials announced the exercise was a success. "You in Alberta," said a Canadian military spokesperson, "have set an example for all of Canada to follow."

Meaning, it must be assumed, that most people should stay at home during an evacuation. That's what actually happened in Calgary.

Operation Lifesaver leaders concluded that ten thousand people out of thirty thousand had participated, a fair amount considering the weather.

If that was true, it's difficult to see where they all went. Small town after small town reported disappointing numbers of evacuees. In Innisfail 336 people in 84 cars showed up, out of an expected 3,500 people. "I think our 218 workers would be a lot happier … if more evacuees had shown up," said Frank Churchill, chairperson of the civil defence committee.

In Crossfield, one-quarter of the expected number showed up, and the curling rink and school were left empty.

Acme prepared for 900 people and got 97. Beiseker took in 168 people, not the expected 1,500. In Strathmore, only 299 of an expected 2,500 Calgarians showed up.

The small numbers and the fact many people left even before the all-clear was given at 3:30 p.m. "left a dubious effect as to the results of the test," wrote one *Herald* reporter.

Particularly disappointing was the fate of the deep-freeze sandwiches in Strathmore, so carefully handled for a week and carefully inspected. "More than half of the 100 loaves of sandwiches were left untouched and Mrs. Fred Hilton was attempting to get rid of them to anyone who wanted them."

Some reporters had quite a bit of fun with the evacuation. Feature writer Ken Liddel's wry look at the civil defence in Bowden noted that although organizers were disappointed with the numbers, the ladies of the town were pleased the legion hall had not been forced into service. They had just cleaned in preparation for a wedding shower that night and feared the result of hundreds of muddy boots tramping across the floor. In the town of Innisfail, the reporter finally found a long lineup, which he assumed was connected with the evacuees. It was, he realized later, a lineup to get into the weekly auction.

Hardest hit by the low numbers, though, were tavern owners, who had stocked up on liquor for the expected hordes of evacuees.

Even in Calgary, there were signs the evacuation didn't quite go as planned. About two hundred people who'd volunteered their cars and driving services for the exercise were turned away, as were three city buses, because there weren't enough people leaving town.

It can only be guessed how many people, being normal Canadians, got the day off work and simply enjoyed themselves. If the film taken by the

National Film Board is any indication, the empty streets of residential northeast Calgary suggest many evacuees went shopping for the day.

Instead of the anticipated ten thousand participants, estimates of actual participation put the figure at about four thousand.

Eventually, the command centre became a storage building and was later demolished. Civil defence plans fell out of favour as Cold War tensions eased. People realized that under a sudden atomic attack, with missiles delivering destruction within minutes, neither hiding in a basement nor attempting to drive two hours out of a city was going to do much good.

Tanks but no tanks

Although not always thought of as a major player on the world scene, Canada was just as worried as other countries during the Cold War, so officials began casting about for a system to protect our troops from enemy aircraft. By the time Canada actually pulled the trigger on the decision and the system was delivered, well, it was 1989; the last of it wasn't delivered until the early nineties. The Cold War was over and the Soviet Union was no longer a monolith.

Still, the world is a dangerous place. And our troops should be protected. So just what did we get to do the job?

Well, the Progressive Conservative government in power at the time did what governments generally do — ignore the real needs of the Canadian Armed Forces for something that will cost lots of money and never be used.

So it considered a system designed by the Swiss company Oerlikon-Buehrle. Now its name — the Air Defence Anti-Tank System, or ADATS — is a bit misleading, suggesting as it does that the system defends against tanks in the air (which are well known to be more heavy and brick-like than aerodynamic), but actually the system is made to shoot down both low-flying aircraft and tanks.

The more analytical among us might wonder what those two things have in common that makes a consolidated defence system a good idea. And the more economical among us might question the practicality of missiles that cost $300,000 each. At that price you might want to try just waving a cheque for $250,000 in front of the tank crew and offering to buy the tank from them, pocketing a handsome $50,000 for yourself.

The ADATS has *some* good points. For example, the ADATS missiles move really fast. They approach Mach 3. That's three times the speed of sound. That's faster than most jets. So they can catch up to a jet without problem. And if they hit one, there won't be much left of the jet.

Of course, if the jets are flying low, which low-flying aircraft generally are, there are frequently trees and buildings and hills and such obstructing the line of sight, so often there just isn't enough time to lock onto them and then "service" them (as military personnel euphemistically term it) with a missile.

The missiles can certainly catch a tank. Tanks move at about sixty kilometres per hour, maximum, on a smooth road, leaving plenty of time for the missiles to lock onto them.

Of course, today's tanks are very heavily armoured. Chobham armour, which is a British invention, is made of layers of steel and ceramic. Even old Soviet-era T-72 tanks — which don't have Chobham armour, just feet and feet of steel plate — are tough. So while the tanks can be caught, there is not a bad chance they can withstand a shot from a kinetic energy weapon like the ADATS — at least from the front.

The armour at the back end of a tank is much thinner, so if the ADATS could hit it from behind, it would be game over for the tank. Of course, to do that, the ADATS would probably have to go behind enemy lines. And the ADATS is not heavily armoured. If it were hit from the right angle, an assault rifle or a rocket-propelled grenade could shoot it up.

The ADATS also has an anti–air radar dish, which makes it tall. And therefore difficult to hide behind enemy lines.

In fact, the ADATS is so tall, the military had to create a "clenching kit" to make the ADATS shorter for shipping. The kit bolts onto the bottom of the chassis and clenches the torsion bars to make it lower.

Unfortunately, because the ADATS is so heavy, the corroded loading ramps on the Hercules cargo aircraft that carry the ADATS overseas have to be buffed up to take the weight, which means the ADATS, even clenched, is too tall to fit on.

And given that our troops need protection overseas, there's not much point in keeping the ADATS in Canada. Its range is ten kilometres. At that rate, we can't even shoot past our territorial waters.

So, thanks to the Cold War — and typical government decision-making — what we ended up with is a system that can destroy a jet but has challenges locking on to it, that can catch a tank but has challenges destroying it, and that isn't really needed at home (which is all to the good, of course) but is too tall to be shipped overseas where it's needed most.

Eventually, the military realized that the missiles are too expensive and not all that effective at disabling a tank, so they ordered ADATS to be used only in an anti-aircraft role. So much for the consolidated defence system.

But it gets better.

The full ADATS system, with missiles and maintenance and all that good stuff, has cost taxpayers about $1 billion — so far.

It's so expensive it is rarely deployed even domestically (although when Canada hosted the G8 Summit in Kananaskis in 2002, it being less than a year after the 9/11 terrorist attacks, the Canadian military actually sent some of the precious anti-air units off to the wilds of Alberta to help protect the G8 leaders against any potential terrorist attack).

The costs have been staggering. It was hoped that the cost to Canada would be defrayed by the Swiss selling the system to other countries, like the United States. But only Canada and Thailand showed interest.

Scott Taylor, perhaps Canada's best military affairs journalist, wrote in his magazine *Esprit de Corp*:

> With no chance to expand their sales, Oerlikon-Buehrle cut their losses and pulled its funding out of the Canadian ADATS program. The result was that the Canadian government alone (read: DND's budget) was left propping up the entire project. With all the start-up costs and research and development factored into the equation, the original 32 units manufactured cost taxpayers over $1 billion — a staggering $30 million per vehicle.
>
> During a 1992 training exercise, a transport trailer carrying an ADATS unit rolled over and crushed the

vehicle's high-tech turret. When DND accountants wrote off the loss, the brass suddenly realized that they couldn't afford to even train with such expensive toys. At that time, all remaining ADATS vehicles were moth-balled at the St-Jean-sur-Richelieu factory, with mainte-nance costs of approximately $40 million per year being paid to Oerlikon.

Well, as long as they've found a good home, right?

Cellphones would have been a lot cheaper

To be a thoroughly modern leader of a thoroughly modern army, you must be thoroughly willing to spend a lot of money. Not on soldiers. Not on vehicles or aircraft or ships.

Everyone has those.

What you need is the latest gizmo. Because if you don't get it, the bad guys will.

That kind of thinking has turned Canada's army into one of the most modern ever.

We've a long history in Canada of trying out new technology for warfare. Fans of our previous book will recall Canadians developed a shovel with a hole in it for the First World War and a ship made of ice for the Second World War.

As the old millennium drew to a close and the new one dawned, the Department of National Defence upheld Canada's military spending tra-dition, purchasing two supply vessels in 1987 for $10 million. A good deal because, Defence officials said, the vessels were in "excellent condition." Imagine how much more excellent they were after Defence had to keep the vessels off the water for a year and spend $16 million to repair them.

And in 1991, recognizing that communication is the lifeblood of the military, Defence spared no expense in contracting out for a long-range communications system. Actually, it was a *very* long range communica-tions system, thereby earning the acronym VLRCS. In military terms, this was not to be confused with the VVLRCS (the very, very long range communication system) or the SOLRCS (sort of long range communication system).

The VLRCS would use satellites and specialized equipment on the ground to allow soldiers to communicate with commanders and each other. The system cost about $174 million.

Meanwhile, the current radio equipment was so outdated, the department had to lease commercial gear to keep our peacekeeping forces going while the new system was being built. At some point over the next few years, it occurred to someone that the commercial system, leased off the shelf, was doing a fine job.

"Here's an idea, and it's just an idea," that someone said during a meeting about the project in 1995. "Why don't we stop building the new system and just use the one we got off the shelf?"

Nope, was the consensus.

That was the only sign of dissent. There may have been others questioning the new system but any objections were lost in the bureaucratic maze.

In the first place, the committee overseeing the project never really had a clear idea of what it wanted out of the system. Although it was worth a lot of money on its own, the VLRCS was part of a much bigger project. In bureaucratese, the bigger project (called the Tactical Command, Control and Communication System) was considered an umbrella project. That meant the individual components were not reviewed on their own. In case you care, it should have been driven as an omnibus project, although it had nothing to do with transportation.

To make matters even more complicated — remember, this is the army and the government we're talking about here — the group overseeing the project and getting half of the technology, called the Information Management Group, was not really communicating (irony of ironies considering what they were building) with the group that was going to get the other half of the technology in the field, called the army.

Meanwhile, the federal government began cutting away at the Defence budget. So the system was changed again, even as it was being built.

Finally, in 1997, the VLRCS was completed. Ta-da! It took another two years for Defence to take delivery of the system, as it figured out how to handle a growing mess. Not only was the commercial system working well and at a lower cost, the VLRCS would require fifty more people to operate it and another $15 million to bring it up to new technical standards.

Defence did the only thing it could do. Out of the $174-million project, only about $10 million in equipment was put in the field. The rest of the stuff, costing $164 million, was put in storage. It has since been renamed the VVECS, the Very, Very Expensive Closet Stuff.

I spy with my little ... wait, where's my laptop?

Oh, those spy movies! They make life in the intelligence service look glamorous and perhaps even a little risky. People in the service have to be always on the alert, always aware of the importance of their work and how dangerous it could be for information to fall into the wrong hands. Or phone booth.

Canada's intelligence services have a sometimes less than stellar record at protecting important information. For example:

- In 1996 a Toronto man — hoping only to make a phone call — found a treasure trove of secret information in a downtown public phone booth. In the booth, sitting on the little brushed metal shelf, was a diskette. It was scratched and not what you would call pristine, so he suspected it had fallen out of a case. There was no information on it about who owned it, so, trying to be helpful, he left a note in the phone booth that he'd found the disk there and gave his phone number. No one called. Finally, he popped it into his computer to see if there was information on it that might give him a clue as to who owned it. Luckily he didn't need to hack into it, or buy special security breaking software to open the encrypted files inside, or even use a secret decoder ring.

  "It came up without any conversion. It just opened right up; it wasn't password protected and [as] I started scanning through this stuff there was a large quantity of clearly sensitive information. Quite frankly, I thought at first it was just an elaborate practical joke. It was a whole bunch of cloak-and-dagger stuff."

In the *Globe and Mail* story on the incident, by Andrew Mitrovica and Jeff Sallot, Peter Marwitz, a former CSIS officer, said the case of the missing diskette is known widely within the service and is a source of anger for many veteran officers who think the — oh, resist the urge to call it stupidity — large-scale carelessness should have been a firing offence. The agent in question received a two-week suspension. Apparently she was in the process of transferring from Ottawa to Toronto and was taking her files with her on diskettes. Agents no longer physically move files when they're transferred.

Meanwhile, in the House of Commons, the Liberal government of the day tried to brush the incident off. Jean Chrétien tried to defuse the situation with one of his classic methods: humour. Even government secrets greet the light of day in a free society, opined Jean. As you might imagine, that didn't sit well with the opposition parties, who opined that the "incredible blunders of CSIS agents have discredited all Canada's secret services" and made them an "international laughingstock."

- A Vancouver agent was transferred to Ottawa, the nation's capital, after losing information about a subject he was tailing. (Hey, maybe it's in a phone booth somewhere.)

- One of the service's senior officers took her work laptop with her on her holiday. One might think this was a sign of dedication to her job. Well, not exactly. She left the laptop — which contained sensitive intelligence information — in the trunk of her vehicle while she was at a hockey game in another city. The laptop was stolen. Recognizing the importance of the loss, the agent, well, waited several days after returning from vacation before reporting that the laptop might be missing.

She said she waited because she wasn't sure where she'd left the laptop. It could have been in the office. She looked around the house for about a week before informing her bosses what had happened. And when she and her husband, a policeman, did call in the theft, they didn't tell anyone what was on the laptop they reported missing or maybe not missing. The agent said she didn't think it was a big deal because this type of thing had happened before.

As it turned out, three drug addicts had broken into the vehicle (a minivan — not quite the glamorous sports cars you see in spy movies) in a smash-and-grab and then ran off with the laptop. It wasn't CSIS that tracked down the thieves. That was just plain old-fashioned police work. The thieves hadn't thought there was anything of value on the laptop so they chucked it in a dumpster.

· In 1995, CSIS teamed up with the Royal Canadian Mounted Police. It wasn't always a smooth collaboration — one team project, called Sidewinder, ended up going sideways. The initial investigation into the possible influence of Asian Triad crime organizations and the Chinese government in Canadian business and finance caused the RCMP to call for even more scrutiny of the situation. But CSIS officials decided the Sidewinder report was based on little more than conspiracy theories. The report was supposed to be buried and replaced by a revised version called Echo, which CSIS claimed was more accurate and critics claimed was watered down because of political pressure.

The RCMP complained about how CSIS had handled the Sidewinder investigation, but the Security Intelligence Review Committee, an intelligence watchdog, ruled in CSIS's favour, saying: "The Committee found no evidence of political interference as alleged.... Project Sidewinder was not terminated; it was delayed when its product was found to be inadequate.... With respect to the first Sidewinder draft report, we found the draft to be deeply flawed in almost all respects."

So did CSIS effectively bury the deeply flawed report? Well, not exactly. In 2000 excerpts from it were slipped to the *Globe and Mail,* and then the full report was slipped to the *London Free Press.* And, despite finding that CSIS had acted appropriately in the matter, the Security Intelligence Review Committee noted, "The Service [CSIS] disposed of what it regarded as 'transitory documents' related to the Sidewinder first draft report. It is unable to locate other documents the Committee regards as clearly non-transitory and has stated that these were not disposed of but rather 'misfiled.'"

But if CSIS is getting tired of having its top-secret information discovered by reporters and rank amateurs, it could resort to the more direct do-it-yourself method. Like in 1999 when it learned that some of its agents were disclosing secret information — on the Internet.

What? I was in the army to fight?

Pity, and celebrate, the life of Louis du Port Chambon, Sieur de Vergor, surely the Failing Founding Father of Canada.

His incompetence almost single-handedly changed the course of history in the new land, not once, but twice. The second time led to the most drastic change in power ever in Canada.

Born in France to a soldiering father, he was raised in Louisbourg in New France and worked his way up the military hierarchy. His rise was aided by the family's friendship with the corrupt Intendant Francis Bigot in Quebec. In 1754, Vergor was given command of the small but key Fort Beausejour, near Sackville, New Brunswick, one of two forts that controlled the Isthmus of Chignecto connecting Nova Scotia to the mainland. Besides defending the fort from the English, he was advised by Bigot to make sure both of them got a good cut from the supplies he ordered for the fort.

Vergor must have spent most of his time working out ways to make money, because by the time British forces started gathering nearby in the summer of 1775, it was clear that he had done little to reinforce either the fort or the surrounding area. British forces attacked on June 16, 1755. Well, it was sort of an attack. One cannon shell found its way into the fort and exploded. Vergor, with about 160 regular soldiers and some less-than-enthusiastic Acadian settlers, facing about 2,500 English soldiers and with nothing to protect them but an un-reinforced fort, surrendered instantly, without firing a shot.

The next day Benjamin Rouer de Villeray surrendered the other key post, Fort Gaspereau, also without being attacked. Acadia collapsed and the British started rounding Acadians up and deporting them to the U.S. seaports.

Vergor faced a court martial but Bigot's influence saved him. Having failed miserably at a small but key fort, he was given a command of about one hundred men in Quebec City in the midst of the Seven Years War that pitted, among many other European powers, England against France. By 1759, the English naval forces under General James Wolfe had moved down the St. Lawrence River to camp outside the great power of New France, Quebec City. Surrounded by rivers and rising in two levels on a cliff up to sixty metres high, Quebec was a natural fortress, so Vergor's command should not have been demanding.

General Quebec military commander Louis-Joseph de Montcalm simply had to wait out the English ships that came down river until winter froze them or they fled to warm water. Major General James Wolfe, the British commander, had to figure out a way to get up those cliffs to the land around Quebec.

On July 20, Wolfe tried storming the cliffs by landing on the Beauport Shore below. Hundreds were cut down by French musket fire from above. A sudden rainstorm turned the cliffs into a mudslide and many soldiers fell to their death. The English were forced to retreat, losing 443 men out of 800 to death or injury.

The huge defeat sent Wolfe to bed sick with worry for ten days. He came up with a new and desperate plan. He had learned of a small, overgrown path that led to the top of the cliffs just a few miles west of Quebec City. On the night of September 13, 1759, British troops scaled the cliff up the path.

Commanding the troops at the top of the path was, of course, Vergor. He had one hundred men at his disposal, probably enough to pick off the

British and send for help. But Vergor had sent most of his men, about seventy, back home to pick their crops. He was asleep. The shots awoke him and he rushed to the top of the path with about thirty men.

It was too late. The British gained the cliff and engaged the French on the Plains of Abraham. The British won. New France became British colonies. The British colonies to the south were allowed to thrive in peace, until they overthrew the British, of course. Quebec became a province surrounded by an English-speaking country.

While running away, Vergor was shot in the ankle. He sailed back to France in 1761 and retired from the army in 1764. He died sometime after 1775. In retirement he received a pension from the army. It was money well spent just to keep him out of active service.

CHAPTER 6

BUSINESS

You've got to spend money to make money. In Canada, sometimes you've got to keep spending and spending and spending. Then bail.

Great Expectations in a Tale of Two Cities

Charles Dickens, the English novelist whose characters often held names that suggested their character traits and that rolled off the tongue, would have loved the moniker Count Andrezej von Staufer. The name looks and sounds imperial and noble and perhaps just a little suspect.

Much like the idea that had Ontario politicians in twelve cities salivating in the late eighties — a $100-million, twenty-five-acre Charles Dickens theme park.

That's right, a theme park based on the abject poverty, injustice, and class warfare that pervaded Dickens's works.

Whee! Jump aboard the Oliver Twister. Watch out for pickpockets.

Have fun in the Bleak House!

Line up for the gruel ride! Wait, the lineup is the ride.

Always a happy ending, but mind the rats on the way.

Apparently, the potential fun was enough to convince twelve Southern Ontario cities to reply to von Staufer's original invitation in 1988. Of the twelve, von Staufer narrowed it down to four — Stratford, Hamilton, Burlington, and St. Catharines.

When residents of London, Ontario, found out, they were a tad miffed. After all, London, Ontario, had a Thames River, dozens of other London, England, namesakes, a castle-like building on the river, and a Storybook Gardens.

London, von Staufer said, sent no more than a couple of tourist brochures in reply to his request for information. Nobody in London's economic office could remember his invitation, but they scrambled to make up for it. "Obviously we're interested," said Ray Jenkins, economic development co-ordinator.

Hamilton scoffed. "We've been told we have the inside track," said its tourism manager, Gabe Macaluco. The regional government of Hamilton had already picked several sites and would have "no problem" getting investors, he said.

Stratford was lukewarm on the idea. It already had a giant tourist attraction, the Stratford Festival, which didn't rely on a Shakespeare theme park.

If you drive this car too much, you will go blind

Every few years, Canadian companies have to relearn something about Quebec. That something being that people speak French in Quebec. Not only that, they speak French slang in Quebec. What you think is a good name in Quebec may not be.

Hunt-Wesson bakeries found that out when it introduced a product line called Big John in Quebec. It seemed only natural to translate Big John literally. The products were sold as Gros Jos. In Quebec slang, that translated into big breasts. Sales did not suffer.

In 2003, General Motors Canada learned the same lesson the hard way. The automobile company wanted to rename its Buick Regal as the Buick LaCrosse. U.S. focus groups liked the name and said LaCrosse gave the car a sophisticated European air. Quebec focus groups just giggled and snorted. Among Quebec youth especially, *lacrosse* is slang for masturbation.

"It also means 'I just got screwed', or 'I just got taken'," said Steve Low, a GM Canada spokesperson at the time.

An unnamed GM vice-chairman was quoted in the *National Post* expressing his feeling of being let down by his own education.

"I speak French as taught in Switzerland and as taught in France, I spent three years in Paris functioning in the French system, and I thought I knew every expression existing in the French language for self-gratification, including the crudest ones known to man," said the chairman. He did not explain why he learned every expression in the French language for masturbation.

GM wanted no French slang attached to its car, although there was probably a sharp GM marketing executive keen on the idea. What could be easier than selling a car with a name that meant self-gratification? Isn't that what car makers have actually been selling for years?

St. Catharines was waiting for more information.

Meanwhile, Londoners, the Ontario ones, learned Mayor Tom Gosnell had indeed received a letter about the theme park back in May but failed to pass it on to the economic development department.

Probably, Gosnell told reporters, because the theme park is a hoax. The address on the letterhead of the Ephemera Society said Wassail House, which means it's a Welsh pub, he said. Calls to the theme park headquarters got only an answering machine.

Over the next few weeks, the mystery and scandal deepened. Ontario's cultural attaché in London, England, remembered discussing the count's idea. A newspaper editor in Cardiff, Wales, confirmed that the count was indeed a real count and a real person whose main hobby was collecting Christmas paraphernalia from around the world. The address was from an ordinary residential area, he said. It's also quite common for people in Britain to name their houses, he pointed out.

A design concept company called Leisure World International confirmed it was seeking a spot in North America for Dickensworld and that the count had been hired as a consultant. Leisure World had already designed a Santa's Village in Sweden and was working on a Spanish theme park based on the fairy tales of Hans Christian Andersen, company officials said.

The count himself refuted claims he lived in a pub. "Rubbish, it's pure rubbish. I don't think I've had a drink all year."

You could hear London, Ontario, residents groan as far away as London, England.

What an opportunity slipping through their fingers. The theme park would create dozens of spinoff businesses all based on a Dickens theme, the company's manager said.

Company officials toured southern Ontario in January 1989. It was London's last chance.

To London's disappointment, in early February 1989, Hamilton was chosen as the site for the theme park. The victory was short-lived.

A few months passed, and Hamilton officials heard nothing from the European leisure company. Apparently, Leisure World could not get investors interested in shelling out $100 million for a theme park based on Dickens.

"It just kind of died," said Jenkins, Hamilton's economic development co-ordinator.

Well, what did they expect out of Dickens? Somebody always dies.

If you feel guilty, act guilty

In order to distinguish oneself in the world of bad marketing, one has to turn to beer. Lots of it.

In 1963, Dow Breweries launched a new beer in Quebec called Kebec. The name was supposed to inspire nationalism, with the Canadian flag thrown into the campaign. Instead, people complained about the use of sacred symbols in a beer campaign. Dow was forced to stop the campaign after just fifteen days.

The brewery recovered from that mistake and by 1966 was the number one brand in Quebec, helped along by one of those catchy rhyming slogans that epitomized branding in the sixties, "Wouldn't a Dow go good now?" And the answer in another slogan, "Now for Dow."

Then sixteen men in the Quebec City area died of a degenerative heart disease that was thought to be linked to beer. Why? Well, the men did drink a lot of beer, eight quarts a day. That was all the evidence there was. Given that the men drank mostly Dow, it could appear that Dow killed the men. There wasn't any proof, and Dow could have ridden out the potential scandal simply by proving there wasn't a link. The company went as far as testing their product to prove there was nothing wrong with it.

Then, for some reason, Dow decided to shut down the Quebec City brewery and dump all Dow Ale into the St. Lawrence River. About a million gallons, worth $625,000, flowed down the river and into the Atlantic Ocean. That begged the question in the minds of consumers: if Dow wasn't guilty of something, then why was it dumping all its beer into the river?

A few months later, Dr. Yves Morin of the Quebec Institute of Cardiology announced that Quebec breweries were adding cobalt to their beer to improve the "head" at the same time the deaths occurred. Dow had been using more of the additive than the other breweries.

The breweries were ordered not to use cobalt anymore and no new cases of degenerative heart disease occurred.

Although no testing proved Dow beer caused the heart disease, Dr. Morin's conclusions and the dumping of the beer made people in Quebec think twice about having a Dow now. Molson and Labatt started outselling Dow. Dow plants in Quebec and Ontario were closed, and in 1973 Molson bought out Dow.

In a bit of irony, about thirty years after Dow got in trouble for using nationalism to sell beer, Molson launched its "I am Canadian" campaign. This time, linking beer to patriotism was easy for Canadians to swallow.

In a further bit of irony, in 2005 the "I am Canadian" beer company was bought by U.S. beer giant Coors.

Gold rush in, gold rush out

Things not to trust in the middle of a gold rush:

- The newspapers.
- The prospectors.
- The banks.
- The government.
- Experts.
- The gold itself.
- And finally, any gold rush town that gives itself an over-the-top promising name, such as, let's say, Eldorado.

The area around Hastings County in Ontario, which stretches from Lake Ontario north into shield country, had been prospected and mined for iron ore, copper, and other minerals since the 1820s.

Searching for copper in the unseasonable cold of August 16, 1866, farmer and part-time prospector Marcus Powell was working on the Richardson family farm when he struck something even better — a seam of gold. No wait, look farther — a cave of gold.

"The gold was found in all these rocks in the form of leaves and nuggets and in the roof it ran through foot thickness like knife blades," he recalled years later. "The largest nugget was about the size of a butternut."

From the humble beginnings of the mine shack shown here came the creation of the town of Eldorado and the rush of thousands to the area in search of gold.

At first Powell and his partners couldn't believe what they had, but a geologist doing a survey in the area confirmed the discovery.

The rush had begun! Eventually. First word had to filter up through the local papers to the big-city *Belleville Intelligencer* and *Hastings Chronicle*.

That took until October, but the papers made up for lost time in hyperbole. "Rich, not only rich in the ordinary sense of the term, but very rich," wrote Belleville's *Weekly Intelligencer* on October 26, 1866. "There is no humbug in the discovery. The great question of interest is does it exist in quantities."

A week later, the answer seemed certain. The gold could extend from the area just north of Lake Ontario all the way to Georgian Bay.

Experienced miners from British Columbia, California, and Australia examined the gold find and said it looked just like the formations of the huge gold fields in those places.

"A new California at our very doors," the *Intelligencer* suggested.

Hundreds of prospectors and the simply curious began flooding to the Powell mine and farms throughout the area, Madoc Township, to determine how much gold there was. Farmers dropped their plows and took up picks on their land. "Experts" arrived in Belleville and the community of Madoc to give speeches on geology before hundreds of gold-hungry spectators. At least one surveyor made a good living from selling maps of the gold veins in the area for $1 apiece. Both Belleville, the closest train stop, and Madoc, the closest town, dreamed in gold.

By 1867, a plan for a town near the Richardson farm was drawn up and given the name Eldorado, after the mythical town of gold in Southern America. The name seemed appropriate. Reports spread that the ore from the Richardson mine was yielding an amazing $12,000 of gold each ton. By the end of the year, Eldorado was a boom town of eighty buildings.

In nearby Madoc, busy property owners turned houses and other buildings into boarding houses for the miners who were expected to flood in come spring. Prices for lumber and food shot up. The two-horse stage from Belleville to Madoc turned into a full line, with eight four-horse coaches delivering prospectors in about three and a half hours. A steamer started making regular trips from Rochester across Lake Ontario to Brighton, where another new stage line brought more fortune hunters to Madoc. Everyone could make money.

It didn't take long for the initial excitement to fade. There actually wasn't a lot of gold to be found. Out of three hundred shafts dug, fewer than one hundred turned up gold. Many of the one- or two-man prospector outfits left. But that wasn't going to hurt Eldorado or Madoc, because huge new companies that could process the ore and still make workers and investors rich had started setting up shop near the mines that did show some trace of gold.

These days, the one-word company name holds sway over the minds and pocketbooks of investors: Nike, Apple, Microsoft. In the 1800s, though, it was important to have an impressive, official-sounding name. And so the Provincial Mining Company, the El Dorado Mining Company, the Wellington Gold Mining Company of Madoc, Bay State Mining Company, and the Anglo-Saxon Gold Mining Company invested money in mines and processing plants, such as the Gold and Silver Reduction Works, using equipment such as the Excelsior Gold Crusher.

The gold continued to show promise. The Gold and Silver Reduction Works in Eldorado was taking an average of about $40 dollars in gold out of each ton from various mines. Sure it was a far cry from the $12,000 per ton rumoured in the early days, but gold was gold, no matter how much came out and how hard it was to separate it from the quartz.

Or so everyone thought. It began to surface that the ore left over after the easy-to-dig stuff had been assessed wasn't giving up its gold as easily. The gold under the ground in Hastings County was contained in a kind of ore from which it was difficult to extract the treasure.

Eight mills had been built by 1868. None of them could get enough gold out of the ore to make the effort worthwhile. All of them shut down. The Richardson Gold Mining Company itself struggled on for two more years, then closed in 1869.

Perhaps $500,000 in capital, machinery, and wages was put into the ground. Perhaps $100,000 in gold came out. More than four thousand gold-hungry people had passed through the area, but only ten years later, Madoc returned to its sleepy self and Eldorado's streets of gold returned to grass.

Those cute puppies bite the hardest

Aw, the cute little puppy. The cute little fuzz puppy. What could be more cuddly and safe and happy than a fuzz puppy?

Born in the seventies, the fuzz puppy, which looked a bit like a raggedy Scottie dog, was designed to cover tissue boxes.

Late in the decade that taste forgot, an Atlanta company named Formar America was popping out fuzz puppies by the thousands. Everyone wanted one. Everyone forgot that all puppies, even toothless tissue box ones, like to bite.

Thousands of kilometres away from Atlanta, in London, Ontario, a group of about one hundred investors, mostly doctors, decided to pool their money together and invest it in something.

They consulted the man who looked after their life insurance and registered retirement plans, a James Sylvester.

At first they were going to set up just one company called Med Unlimited. The province of Ontario, though, came up with a scheme that gave tax-free grants to investors on 30 percent of the money they put up. So the doctors and Sylvester set up at least two more companies to get even more of the tax-free grants.

James E. Sylvester Diversified Inc. was set up to manage the affairs of the new companies.

Sylvester later testified at his trial for fraud that he had long-term plans for investing in real estate but also need "quick cash generators" to pay the interest on debts incurred from starting up those long-term plans.

One of those quick cash generators was the fuzz puppy. This was the era of the pet rock, so anything could sell if marketed well. The company that made the puppies, Formar, projected sales of 2.2 million fuzz puppies, with a profit of $1 to $1.50 per puppy.

The money started to pour into the fuzz puppy operation from Sylvester's investors, the doctors, and from the vice-president of London's District Trust Co., Roland Bobbie, who also knew a good thing when he saw it. The trust company provided about $4 million in loans to Sylvester, which sent most of that money to Formar to make fuzz puppies. At one point, District Trust was feeding the fuzz puppy operation $50,000 a week in loans.

The trust company also provided about $11 million in individual loans to members of Sylvester Inc., some of that money going to the other companies. Those loans were secured by the mortgages and other assets of the good doctors. And just to make sure it wasn't left out of the fuzz puppy craze, District Trust also invested its own money, about $159,000, into the three Sylvester-run companies.

Everything was working fine. The shelves of the Atlanta plant were filling up with fuzz puppies. District Trust's Vice-President Roland Bobbie, James Sylvester, and Sylvester's accountant all travelled to Atlanta in April 1980. There were shelves and shelves of the puppies. There were no orders yet, but they would come. By Christmas, everyone would want a fuzz puppy under the tree.

Then the recession hit North America. And, perhaps, a bit of taste.

The fuzz puppies were left on the shelves, cold and unwanted. About $2 million in stock was liquidated for $599,000.

The London doctors lost hundreds of thousands of dollars. The $15 million that District Trust lent to Sylvester Inc. was gone. In 1981, after posting huge losses, the trust company went under. To be fair, in the eighties dozens of Canadian trust companies went under, but District was the only one that collapsed because of tissue box fuzz puppies.

After two and a half years of investigating, police laid 238 charges against Sylvester, Bobbie, and a third man.

Sylvester was cleared on thirty-two charges of fraud and theft. The doctors, ruled the judge, were big boys who knew what they were getting into. However, he did find Sylvester guilty of defrauding the provincial government for using one relatively small $857,000 grant. He was fined $20,000.

Bobbie was first convicted of fraud and sentenced to eighteen months in jail. But that conviction was appealed, and at a trial less than three years later, charges were dismissed. And charges were withdrawn against the other man.

At Bobbie's first trial, the fuzz puppies finally got their proper promotion. What one reporter described as a gaudy, shaggy, flashy red and white version was put on display before a judge. The judge seemed "less than enchanted" with the red version, the reporter noted. You think this is bad, the prosecutor told the judge, you should have seen the orange and green ones.

Every business has its ups and downs

David Gilmour had a problem.

Actually, he had many problems. His lumber mill was in Trenton, Ontario, and the new timber rights he had just paid almost $750,000 for, in 1890 dollars, was 445 kilometres away to the north in what is now Algonquin Park near Dorset.

There was a series of creeks, swamps, lakes, and rivers that Gilmour would have to divert, dam, and manipulate to get his logs from Algonquin to Trenton. Solving the problem of waterways that weren't built for log drives would take hard work, but it wasn't anything your typical lumberman couldn't solve with a lot of men and money.

No, what really stumped, so to speak, Gilmour was a 1.8-kilometre stretch of land that rose thirty-five metres between one body of water, Lake of Bays, and another body of water, a canal he had built into Raven Lake. The rise of land stood at the northern end, or beginning, of his log drive. If he couldn't get logs over the land, there was no way of getting them to his mill in Trenton.

So Gilmour devised an ingenious way to move the logs uphill, a combination of jack ladders and slides. Jack ladders used steam engines to drive a cleated chain, which dug into the bark and carried logs up inclines. Slides used water to push logs when the land went downhill. At the Lake of Bays, one jack ladder, about sixty metres long, carried logs twelve metres up to the first slide. The same steam engine that drove that jack ladder also drove a pump that carried water from the Lake of Bays up to the first slide. The water pushed logs through a wooden trough to the second jackrabbit. The second jackrabbit was really eight jackrabbits, working in tandem to carry logs 27 metres up over a distance of 762 metres.

After that, the logs would finally be in the canal that took them the rest of the way.

It took nearly five hundred men months of hard work in 1893 to build the tramway and one hundred men to run the machinery and handle the logs at transfer points. The system cost Gilmour about $150,000. It looked like a brilliant investment in the spring of 1894, when the tramway began carrying logs from one waterway to the next. But the logs were moving in single file, about eighty metres a second.

Gilmour had hoped to move 10,000 logs a day to feed his hungry mill. Historians Gary Long and Randy Whiteman (authors of several books on the tramway and the source of this account) figure the contraption was averaging just 2,700 logs a day. Part of the problem was the mechanics of a long and complicated series of machinery. The longer the logs took to get through the tramway, the longer they took to get to the waterways. The delay was a problem since water levels fell in fall. During the first year of the tramway's operation, not a single Algonquin log made it to the mill. Some of those logs had been cut two years earlier.

Gilmour refused to be disheartened. He had even more trees in the Algonquin area cut, and in the spring of 1895 he began a new log drive. That summer, maybe three thousand logs a day made it through the tramway. Aside from the usual breakdowns, water levels were low even north of the tramway. That meant that it took even longer to get the logs to the tramway, so by the time the logs hit the slides, the water levels were even lower because of the lateness of the season. By fall, only thirty-five thousand logs had made it to the mill. The rest were stuck at various points along the route. The good news was that the logs driven the year before had finally made it to Trenton. The bad news was they were pretty beat up and pretty waterlogged. And many showed signs of rot. To add to the problems of lower quality wood driven 445 kilometres at high cost, the lumber market started to fall.

The tramway lasted one more year before Gilmour pulled the plug on the machinery and the water slides. He soon got out of the lumber business and concentrated on making doors.

CHAPTER 7

FARMING

It should be easy to find a spot to farm in Canada. Rule out all the places with too much snow, or too many bugs, or too cold weather, or too hot weather, and you're left with few choices. But we Canadians are made of foolhardier stock than that. Often backed by our well-meaning political masters, we like to try making a living where we shouldn't or in ways we shouldn't.

Pulling the wool over everyone's eyes

Sheep.

They were on Governor George Simpson's mind.

No, he wasn't counting sheep in an effort to sleep. He was counting on sheep.

Sheep would lead the way. Seriously. Yes, sheep would lead the hard-bitten Red River, Manitoba, colony to economic success.

He wasn't trying to pull the wool over anyone's eyes.

By 1832, the settlers of Red River had spent up to two decades battling the elements, the geography, poor supply of goods, and stupidity. More settlers in Canada were hurt or killed by the stupidity of others than by just about anything else.

And in this case, the damage didn't stop with the good people of Red River. But it *did* start with them.

Simpson, governor of the Hudson's Bay Company, had turned to Robert Campbell for help. Campbell was of Scottish origin, born the son of a successful sheep farmer in Glenlyon, Perthshire, Scotland, on February 21, 1808. Campbell arrived at the Red River colony in 1832 at Simpson's invitation. His job was to run the sheep farm being started by the HBC at St. James Parish, on the Assiniboine River, a few miles west of where the city of Winnipeg is today.

Governor Simpson was not short on energy, or ideas, although not all were gems. (For example, he vigorously promoted the Buffalo Wool Company; see the next story for more sad details.)

He started an experimental farm on the Assiniboine. After six years of effort the farm failed: cost to the company was £3,500 sterling. He attempted a farm for growing flax and hemp. The flax grew and the hemp grew and then both crops rotted in the fields. An expensive flax mill built to manufacture the product fell into decay.

With the thousands of British pounds wasted, you could call them sterling examples of failure.

But the sheep idea was solid, right? He brought in a Scottish sheep farmer to run things. And running a sheep farm in Manitoba can't be that different from running one in Scotland.

The first thing to do was get some sheep. There were no sheep in Manitoba, but Missouri was selling sheep cheap. So Robert Campbell, Glen Rae, another Scot, John Bourke, an Irishman, and a handful of other men went to Missouri. But the Missourians wanted way too much for the sheep. Originally they asked for ten shillings a head for the sheep. This was two or three shillings more than Rae thought was fair. Eventually the Missourians offered the sheep at seven shillings and change, but Rae, offended, refused the offer.

They headed east — 450 miles east to Kentucky, where they saved a few pennies a head for their trouble.

They bought 1,475 sheep and headed home. Of course, Manitoba is a long way from Kentucky. And sheep have short legs. They're not renowned for their speed. Travelling back, the herders had to pay for the sheep to be fed. This quickly ate up any savings they made by going to Kentucky.

To make some money, they offered to shear the sheep and sell the wool to a business on the Mississippi on their way back to St. Louis. A price was agreed on and the sheep were sheared and the wool gathered. But the business couldn't raise all of the money. Bitter and cranky, the leaders of the sheep convoy ordered the wool to be burned rather than sold at a lower rate. Poor people in the area offered to buy the wool at rates they could afford, but the group was adamant — if they weren't paid the full price, the wool would be burned. And it was.

By the time they made it back to Missouri, they had travelled nine hundred miles round trip from where they were going to buy the sheep originally. If they had bought the sheep in Missouri, they would have been home by then.

Home they headed, crossing an ocean of dry grass that had hard points capable of poking through the tender skin of the sheep. And it did. Dozens of sheep died as they pushed their way through, becoming more and more exhausted each day. To stop their suffering, the workers slit the throats of the injured sheep. One day, even before breakfast, they had to kill forty-four of the animals. After days of killing hundreds of sheep, they refused to kill any more, leaving the killing to their bosses.

Finally they reached Red River with 251 sheep, the trail behind them marked with the carcasses of 1,200 sheep. Counting them is guaranteed to not put you to sleep.

Miss Smith, get me the buffalo file and a fresh ale

Here's how witness Alexander Ross described the scene: "What scenes of disorder! what waste, what excess and folly! Half the people were off duty, officials as well as others, wallowing in intemperance. One man lying drunk here, an-other there; the bottle and glass set up at every booth, and all com-ers invited to drink free of cost."

No, it wasn't the Senate. Good guess, though.

Ross was describing the daily operations of Manitoba's Buffalo Wool Company, set up by several entrepreneurs in 1825.

The idea seemed foolproof. Trying to raise sheep in the Red River area was difficult because there were so many wolves. On the other hand, buffalo seemed to thrive. Therefore, all one had to do was kill buffalo, gather the wool and hides, process them, and ship them off to England and local settlements. Then wait for the money to come in.

Wrote Ross, "It was the chairman's belief, to quote his own words, that 'To accomplish these important ends, neither much capital nor much skill was required.'"

A company of like-minded men invested £2,000 and directed all the plainsmen to gather the hides and the women to gather the wool.

However, two "evils" beset the company, Ross wrote.

"First, the wool and the hides were not to be got, as stated, for the picking up; and, secondly, all who had previously applied themselves to the cultivation of the soil, threw aside the hoe and spade to join the plain-rangers."

The "solid reliance of agriculture" was replaced all over the Red River area by "the channel of barbarism." The rising demand for the not-so-easy-to-get buffalo hides and wool drove up the prices the plainsmen demanded.

That didn't bother the investors. They ordered tannery machinery, dyes, and skilled workers from England. They also hired a superintendent, clerk, and storekeeper. From the Red River settlement, the company hired curriers, skinners, wool dressers, and sorters.

And, it being the Wild West, "nothing could be done in those palmy days without the bottle and the glass, spirits were imported by the hogshead."

Employee morale was quite high.

"Money was spent as if the goose that laid the golden eggs was to live for ever," said Ross, clearly not comprehending the importance of high morale. Instead, he took a dim view of the tannery after visiting it himself, writing, "The hides were allowed to rot, the wool spoiled; the tannery proved a complete failure."

He may have been a bit harsh. After all, a few samples of cloth had been made and sent home. So what if the cloth cost twelve pounds ten shillings per yard to make but sold for only four shillings per yard in England? Employee morale was still quite high.

It was also short-lived. The company went under and the investors lost not only their capital but also £4,500 borrowed from the Hudson's Bay Company. The company eventually forgave the loan.

Sir Wilfred Grenfell thought he'd leave a legacy in Newfoundland by importing herds of reindeer. He did. The reindeer died but they left a nasty parasite to kill herds of other animals.

So, the plan is to kill reindeer and caribou

Stop us if you've heard this one before: "This is going to make Newfoundland rich."

No one yet has counted all the schemes proposed over the last four hundred or so years to make the province better off. You could put your hand into almost any era and pick one out. How about this one? The great reindeer experiment.

Three hundred of the beasts were brought to Newfoundland in 1907 by Sir Wilfred Grenfell, a missionary doctor who the rest of the time did a lot of good for the province.

Grenfell himself footed the cost of $14,000 for bringing the reindeer from Norway. It would be well worth the expense, he told skeptics. The reindeer was known in Norway as the horse and cow combined. The females could be milked. Both male and female could pull wagons. And they were good eating, too. As for their own food, they would do well on Labrador moss.

Perhaps, but the reindeer were also an easy target for predators, disease, and parasites that were new to them.

There are two stories about the end of the herd. The more scientific suggests the herd was so thinned out that Grenfell gave up. The rest of the reindeer were put down.

An apocryphal version suggests the herd grew to fifteen hundred reindeer before Newfoundlanders, eager to eat, slaughtered most of them.

In any case, the reindeer did have a long-lasting effect on Canada.

They brought with them a parasite that is fatal to Newfoundland's caribou.

In some places, you can even harvest the mosquitoes

Nothing was going to stop the British from settling all of what is now Ontario.

Once much of the good land in the southern area was settled by the mid-1850s, the government decided to settle the north, a huge tract of land between the lower Ottawa River and Georgian Bay. The measly layer of soil over the Canadian Shield, the huge outcrops of rock poking through the surface as easily as a needle through cotton, the air thick with mosquitoes and blackflies, the long cold winters — oh, the government recognized that there would be difficulties.

"Natural barriers presented by extensive rugged and comparatively barren tracts were such as to be insurmountable to individual enterprise," wrote the Commissioner of Crown Lands for Upper Canada in his report for 1856.

Perhaps the barriers were "insurmountable to individual enterprise," but not to the mighty Upper Canadian government.

The land was simply too good to ignore.

The good climate and soils could support 8 million people, said Agriculture Minister Philip Vankoughnet in one of his pamphlets urging immigrants to come to Upper Canada. All settlers needed to come pouring into the Ottawa-Huron tract were surveyed lots and roads, the government figured.

Thus began what became known as the Colonization Road Scheme, though it's likely that the somewhat judgement-laden word *scheme* was added later. Politicians may think it, but they are rarely honest enough to call their proposals schemes.

Surveyors were sent into the bush and rock to map the roads, then grid lots out of rock and tree and pine needle soil. In some cases, the roads didn't follow natural level ground but the straight lines over swamps and rocky ground drawn on maps by bureaucrats back in York. The lots were surveyed with the same attention to mathematical detail and neglect of soil conditions, creating entire farm parcels that were little more than bog and rock. Crews hacked, burned, hauled, graded, and pounded roads into shape. In all, thirteen main colonization roads were built criss-crossing central and eastern Ontario.

Meanwhile, back in the British Isles, yet another of the frequent economic depressions was forcing people to migrate to the colonies. The Province of Ontario enticed them to head north in 1868 by passing its Free Grants and Homestead Act. The act gave everyone more than 18,100 acres of land for free and the next 100 for fifty cents an acre. If the homesteader had cleared and cultivated fifteen acres and built a dwelling at least sixteen by twenty feet in five years, he could get title to the land.

Free land, a little work … that drew hundreds of migrants from the relatively crowded south and the more than relatively crowded and land poor British Isles.

So up the roads the homesteaders went.

That alone was no easy task. In spring, the mud and swamps made many of the roads impassable. In summer there were potholes. In winter, the best time to travel, there were huge drifts. But up the roads thousands of settlers came, first spilling onto the lots beside the roads and then the lots further back.

Before the inches-deep soil could be fully exploited, the trees had to go. Conveniently enough, the north was full of lumber companies that had paid the province for the right to take those trees. But the lumber companies didn't have enough workers to clear the land. How serendipitous. At the same time the lumber companies were lobbying the province — no doubt mentioning how much money had traded hands for lumber rights — the settlers were moving in. The settlers provided the labour, and, in lucky cases, the lumber camps took the oats grown by the first fortunate settlers.

Some cynical historians suggest the main reason the province undertook the road scheme was to provide the powerful lumber companies with ready labour. Once the pine was gone, well, the useless soil was the problem of the settlers.

Many land agents oversold the value of the land to settlers. The Hastings Road Agency boasted in 1856 there were 900,000 acres of good agricultural land in the township of Hastings. Historian Peter Young points out that in 1963 a soil report of the area suggested fewer than 150,000 acres in the entire county were suitable for farming.

Now, at first, the Colonization Road Scheme seemed a success.

About one thousand people headed up the Hastings Colonization Road in eastern Ontario. By 1860, already 185 of 309 lots along the Addington Colonization Road farther east were settled. Parry Sound along the Great Northern Colonization Road boomed from two thousand people in 1871 to about fifteen thousand. Another ten thousand or so lived on farms outside.

Then reality hit. Even as the province continued to sell the beauty of farming in bogs, settlers were already leaving. In the early 1880s, the government of Canada and the railways began promoting the prairies of Manitoba. It didn't take much for settlers scrabbling out a living on rock to eye the deep soil of the prairies. What were a few more mosquitoes? Some farmers and some communities hung on. Parry Sound, for example, remains a tourist town of about 6,100 people.

But the bush reclaimed hundreds of farms and dozens of towns. What dreams the poor soil didn't kill, railways' bypassing the road towns and government indifference put under. By the early 1900s, most of the communities were already dead or in the last stages of dying. In 1925, provincial land surveyor C.F. Aylsworth travelled the entire length of the Hastings Colonization Road in eastern Ontario. The road once boasted dozens of towns and four hundred settled lots, but Aylsworth discovered that fewer than 25 percent of the land grants were still occupied. Aylsworth wrote a eulogy for the entire scheme and the dreams the roads inspired, and then killed.

"The mute evidence of it all is empty, dilapidated and abandoned houses, barns, orchards, wells, old broken down fences, root cellars and many other similar evidences of having given up the ghost," he wrote. The road, he said, should be called the Trail of Broken Hearts.

New Ontario, same old lies

Ooh, it sounded so nice.

"There is no place in Ontario where bigger crops of hay, roots, barley, peas, oats and wheat can be grown," declared a pamphlet from Temiskaming and Northern Ontario.

"In New Ontario's Great Clay Belt all can strike it rich," declared another. The soil is "capable of producing grain and vegetable crops surpassed nowhere in agricultural Canada."

Only about sixty years after Ontario failed miserably at settling the central part of the province by building colonization roads, it decided to try its luck even farther north.

It wasn't as daft as it seemed. The glaciers had left deposits of till rich in nutrients along a huge swath of land about 120 kilometres south of James Bay. This huge belt of land was about 1,000 kilometres long and 350 kilometres wide — about 30 million acres in all. About half that — 15,680,000 acres — was in Ontario. It was called the Great Clay Belt, bigger than Massachusetts, Connecticut, Rhode Island, New Jersey, and Delaware combined. If it could be farmed, Northern Ontario would become a breadbasket to the world, or at least some of it. The Great Clay Belt would become the Great Food Belt. To make it sound even better, the area was also called New Ontario.

The area first came to the government's attention in a big way in the 1880s as logging companies and surveyors pushed north. Reports of good farmland and the occasional successful settler fed the province's imagination. Yet settlement in the area sputtered along for decades, hampered by the migration of farmers to the Prairies and the slow progress of roads and rails. When the railway did move in, so did people, but mainly to mining towns for good paying jobs. The province didn't seem to mind.

The year 1911 changed all that. Sir Wilfrid Laurier's Liberals signed the Reciprocity Agreement with the United States, basically a free trade agreement. Faced with the threat of losing the Canadian market to Americans, Ontario looked north. If that Great Clay Belt could be settled, there'd be a bigger at-home market for manufacturers.

In 1912, Ontario passed the Northern and Northwestern Ontario Development Act. At first the province simply sold land to developers who could then oversee settlement. That's when the pamphlets and stories, produced by the government-run railway company, started seeing the light of day in the southern parts of the province.

When the First World War came, agricultural production in Europe nearly collapsed as farmers answered the call to battle and farms were ravaged by fighting. The allies looked to Canada for food. Ontario could provide that food and get out of a pre-war depression.

"I want my voice to ring out in an appeal as strong as I can to our agriculturalists in every part and section of the Province to increase their output," Premier William Hearst was quoted as saying in the *Globe* on April 7, 1916.

Once again, Ontario embarked on making the Great Clay Belt the Great Food Belt. Only two weeks after the *Globe* article, the province changed the Northern and Northwestern Ontario Development Act to offer a $25-an-acre loan for clearing land and to help with getting seed and livestock.

A year later, the province offered even more incentives, hoping New Ontario would be filled with returning soldiers eager to make a new life on the farm. The province surveyed hundred-acre lots in six townships about one hundred kilometres west of Cochrane in Northern Ontario. A board was set up to weed out soldiers who weren't fit for the farm.

In a master stroke, the province decided to build a community that would centre the new agricultural area, so homesteaders wouldn't scatter throughout the six townships and then complain about being isolated and leave. The centre of the agricultural breadbasket was to be Kapuskasing.

The area had long been home to fur traders, and when the National Transcontinental Railway, now CN, pushed north in the early 1900s, a station was built where the tracks crossed the river. The station was given the Cree name Kapuskasing, which means "where the river bends."

The province bought 1,280 acres of land west of Kapuskasing in 1914 to build an experimental farm on the clay belt. But war turned the nascent farm into an internment camp for prisoners of war and illegal immigrants. Over the next six years, thousands of internees cleared hundreds of acres of land and built a hospital, barracks, a canteen, a YMCA, a post office, and a supply depot. The internees turned out to be far more effective than the next wave of visitors.

Each returning soldier would be housed in Kapuskasing and paid about $1,200 to $1,500 to clear and plough the front ten acres of all the lots. The soldiers, soon to be settlers, could work the land with horses, wagons, sleighs, ploughs, and other implements provided by the government and put in a central depot.

The province would also build a frame house on each lot, worth about $500 to $700, with the province paying $150 and the soldier the rest. Each soldier could also get a $500 loan from the province.

The first twenty-four men were sent for instruction on farming in June 1917 and arrived in Kapuskasing in July. By the end of the year, twenty-four men had given up and gone home, but forty-six remained working on their farms. More than fifteen frame houses were up. The province had also set up a school and a railway siding to ship goods in and out.

Everything was working out just fine. Except that some men worked harder and better than others at clearing the lots. And the married men were paid more than the single men and the married men with children were paid more than anyone. Hadn't they all risked their lives equally in the war? Plus, the land was hard to clear. The only way to make money was to clear pulpwood, and the promised paper mill in town did not materialize. Aside from all these niggling complaints, there was one more: few soldiers risked their lives just to return home and take more orders.

A delegation from Kapuskasing travelled to Toronto to tell their story in October 1919.

The land simply wasn't farmland, said one delegate, A.J. Gould: "We cannot see how we can ever get along up here."

By the end of 1919, only four more frame houses had been built, bringing the total to nineteen. There was a store and a two-room school and a blacksmith shop and a planing mill. But only 101 soldiers were actually farming. And it had already cost $800,000.

The province, naturally, set up a Commission of Enquiry. The commission's report was as blunt as a plough worn down by rocky land. The entire scheme to settle the Kapuskasing area was a bust. Many of the handpicked farmers were actually city boys from Toronto who knew little about working the land and didn't want to learn. Those who could farm couldn't farm enough to get out of debt from the government loans and government store.

The province decided to ship home anyone who wanted to go, paying them for any cleared acres and buildings put up. Those who stayed got a free horse and harness, grain, transfer to a better farm, and $500. Sixty-one of the just over one hundred settlers came back to Toronto. It cost the province about $77,000 to bring those settlers back and another $14,000 to keep settlers in Kapuskasing.

But Kapuskasing was only a small part of the disaster.

In eight years, from 1912 to 1920, the Northern and Northwestern Development Act and its various programs had put only five thousand settlers in the Great Clay Belt. That's about one settler for every three thousand acres. And it cost about $10 million. Or $2,000 a settler.

Ontario should have learned. It didn't. Twenty years later, the province was gripped by the Depression. When the federal government announced a plan to settle agricultural areas and relieve pressure on cities, Ontario jumped in. Each person would get $200 from the province, $200 from the federal government, and $200 from the local municipality for settling in the Great Clay Belt. Once again the settlers would be hand-picked, and once again most of them were city folk with little experience in farming.

In its wisdom, the province started shipping would-be settlers to the clay belt in late fall and early winter, exactly the worst time to judge a place and start a new life farming. Some of the lots were more rock than soil; some were bogs. Settlers complained about the monthly grocery orders, both the quality and the amount allowed. As a result, in two years only 499 families, 2,480 people, were placed on the land. A provincial official visited 125 of those families. Only 81 wanted to stay.

The depressed economy and the election of a new government, the Liberals, in 1934 spelled the end of the latest clay belt scheme. It cost the province $200,000 to put 600 families on the land under this plan. By 1940, only 316 were still farming.

To the relief of taxpayers, Premier Mitch Hepburn gave the final word on two decades of trying to get the clay belt settled. "We are going out of the business of colonization," he said.

CHAPTER 8

THE GOVERNMENT

It's impossible to fully comprehend just how much money federal, provincial, and municipal governments in Canada have wasted on dumb ideas.

Entire books, royal commissions, and auditor general reports have attempted to untangle the various financial bungles made by politicians and bureaucrats.

There's a grant for some mathematician somewhere who can study these bungles and come up with a formula explaining them all. Something like this: vote-hungry politicians plus money-hungry executives plus job-fearing bureaucrats times the local unemployment rate minus the inefficient opposition parties equals, well, the mathematical equivalent of an infinitely expanding hole.

Every year Canadians wait for the annual report of the federal auditor general. Each report contains a bit of joy and a bit of pain. The joy comes because someone in government got caught doing something stupid. The pain comes when Canadians realize they are paying for the mistake.

Many stories in this book come out of auditor general reports. Here are a few of our favourites.

Just shoot us now; it'd be less painful

Really good ideas don't have to cost a lot. But you can always trust the government to take a good idea and *make* it cost a lot.

Take the gun registry. According to most Canadians, it's a good idea. Register all the guns in the country and give that information to the police and those who need it so that if they are responding to an emergency call they can find out whether guns or ammunition might be at the call site. Even firefighters answering a call would find it useful to know if there is a possibility of shotgun shells exploding from a fire. The registry isn't going to tell you if there are shotgun shells in the house, but if you know there are shotguns, you would be safer if you assumed there were shells there as well.

The gun registry was supposed to cost $2 million: $119 million to run the program set off by registration fees collected totalling $117 million, leaving a cost to the Canadian taxpayers of, yes, $2 million. Not a bad price tag for a worthy endeavour.

Actual cost? Well, we're not sure yet because it's still mounting, but it could come to $1 billion. The good news is that revenues will be higher. Maybe $140 million instead of the measly $117 million predicted. So the cost to taxpayers? About $860 million.

So who did the math on this one? No one knows, but according to the auditor general's report, the Liberal-run government miscalculated the cost of processing licences and registrations. The forms, true to government, um, form, were too complicated. This resulted in 90 percent of applications containing errors and omissions, more than twice what had been predicted. The Justice Department's computer system simply wasn't equipped to handle the task.

And apparently the bureaucrats who came up with the cost estimates and revenue estimates weren't up to the task either.

But we saved thousands in crew costs

In 1982, Fisheries and Oceans Canada decided to replace an aging patrol boat. The old one operated seasonally, but Fisheries wanted one that could patrol farther offshore all year round. For the next eight years the plan for the patrol boat wound its way through the bureaucracy. In 1987, the Treasury Board approved up to $7.6 million to build the boat. Three years later, though, a check of the design showed the boat being built would not float if all of the required surveillance equipment was put on it. Fisheries could have pulled the plug then and there at a nominal cost. Instead, the department pushed on, lengthening the boat in the design stage.

All along, those in charge knew that the bigger boat with the bigger and better equipment would require more people to operate it. But it wasn't until 1991, nine years later, with $700,000 spent on the project already, that Fisheries decided to examine just how much staff and resources it would take to operate the new vessel. The study delivered interesting news. Compared to the costs of running the old seasonal vessel, the new year-round vessel would require a seven-fold increase in staff and a six-fold increase in the annual budget. The only way to accomplish that would be to dry-dock other vessels. And that would decrease surveillance in the area, the opposite of what the new boat was supposed to accomplish.

So Fisheries scrapped the project and paid the shipyard about $264,000 to cover the costs already incurred.

In other words, the department spent $1 million and ten years on a boat that was never built.

Vote Liberal; only we can keep the dead warm

In the past few years, it's been difficult to keep the bungles plaguing the federal Liberals straight. The gun registry. The sponsorship debacle. The $1-billion Human Resources Development Corporation boondoggle. Almost lost in the blur is the heating credit bonanza of 2001.

In the fall of 2000 winds began to blow down from the Arctic. Natural gas and home heating oil prices were rising. Canadians were worried. Politicians were even more worried; an election was coming.

Prime Minister Paul Martin came to our aid. His mini-budget in October gave a one-time benefit of up to $250 a family, or $125 an individual, to lower-income people facing the wolves — or the wind — at the door.

Only days later, Parliament was dissolved for a federal election. The Liberals must have been so worried about Canadians freezing that they panicked. Otherwise, how to explain the fact they did not introduce legislation on the benefits before Parliament was dissolved?

They got their chance to make good after winning the November 27 election. Parliament wasn't sitting any time soon — it would soon be Christmas after all — but the Liberals got an order-in-council to authorize the money for the heating benefits.

Anyone who got a GST credit would get a cheque for the heating bill. On January 31, 2001, about 8.6 million cheques started leaving Ottawa. In two months, $1.459 billion headed for the hinterland.

Unfortunately, using the GST credit wasn't a good way to figure out who should receive the cheques. There really wasn't all that much connection between deserving a GST credit and needing help with heating, especially since the 2001 GST credits were based on 1999 income tax returns.

According to a later auditor general's report, about 75 percent of the households that got the cheques weren't facing higher heating costs at all. Many were heated electrically and the cost of electricity wasn't going up then. Many paid rent that had utilities included. About a million households might have got two cheques because two income earners got the GST credit.

Of the more than $1.4 billion sent out in heating relief cheques, only $250 million to $350 million went to people who faced an immediate hike in heating costs. About ninety thousand desperate people who were facing a heating crunch didn't get a cent.

Among those who did get the heating cheques: at least 4,000 Canadians who did not live in Canada (how many pina coladas will $250 buy?); about 7,500 dead people (in Liberal heaven, you *can* take it with you); and finally, about 1,600 inmates in federal prison (cigarettes on me!).

Work would be so much easier if you didn't have to show up all the time...

Ah, the Senate. Nothing says honour and loyalty like the Canadian Senate. The House of Sober Second Thought. Wait a minute — are you giggling?

Not many hold much respect for senators. The Senate is seen as a big pasture where political cronies are given their rewards. Public service isn't what most people equate with the Senate. So when even senators seem angry at one of their own because of a lack of responsibility, that tells you something.

When the Senate turned on Senator Andrew Thompson in the fall of 1997, it was a surprise. But it shouldn't have been.

Thompson, seventy-three, had attended just 47 of the 1,088 sittings of the Senate in fifteen years. "My attendance record is shocking," admitted Thompson.

He said that in an interview from his winter home in La Paz, Mexico, in February 1998, in response to the Senate's decision to suspend Thompson without his $64,400 pay and other extras.

Apparently he spent a lot of time in La Paz.

Thompson didn't take any responsibility for his treatment at the hands of his peers. He blamed the media. He said he was a victim of "trial by newspaper." He told the press that the role of senators has to be broadened so attendance isn't the only benchmark.

"There seems to be this obsession that you have to sit there."

He also said his colleagues' actions were generated out of fear of being branded as irrelevant.

How much for a return ticket?

Back in 1996, the auditor general took a look at the way the Coast Guard, run by Transport Canada, was buying ships.

In 1992, a Nova Scotia Coast Guard ship needed a refit. A Nova Scotia shipyard and a Newfoundland shipyard both bid on the project. The Newfoundland shipyard's bid was $407 less. It got the contract.

The problem was that it cost $21,000 to get the ship from Nova Scotia to Newfoundland for the repairs.

In 1993 a Newfoundland Coast Guard ship needed a refit. A Newfoundland shipyard and a Nova Scotia shipyard both bid for the project. The Nova Scotia bid was $28,071 lower than the Newfoundland bid. So Transport Canada gave the bid to the Nova Scotia shipyard.

The problem was that it cost $54,500 to send the ship from Newfoundland to Nova Scotia for the repairs.

In 1995, another Nova Scotia Coast Guard ship needed refitting. Again, a Newfoundland shipyard and a Nova Scotia shipyard bid on the project. This time, the Newfoundland shipyard's bid was $71 lower. So, naturally, it got the contract.

The problem was that it cost more than $30,000 to send the Nova Scotia ship to Newfoundland for the repairs.

The auditor general does not explain why it costs less to send a ship from Nova Scotia to Newfoundland than the other way around. However, there was some good news in the auditor general's 1995 report. It appeared that some lights were finally going on in Transport Canada offices.

"An interdepartmental marine working group," the auditor general reported, "has recommended that the department's additional costs of vessel fuel and crew transportation costs be factored into future considerations of contract bids."

You think?

Maybe if they all thought like Thompson, none of them would have been there to kick him out in the first place.

Why couldn't we just let P.E.I. do it?

Fried, broiled, baked, whipped, mashed.

Take all those good words for potatoes and apply them to the plans cooked up by the Saskatchewan government in the nineties to turn part of the province into a mini–Prince Edward Island.

Use all those good words, with more sympathy, for all the ordinary people creamed in that traditional Canadian dish — huge goals, government money, a lack of proper planning, a lack of proper control, and a lack of public knowledge.

The recipe for disaster began with the Saskatchewan government deciding in 1996 that it knew better than farmers what should be grown in the Lake Diefenbaker area. For thirty years the province had been spending money on irrigating the area and offering grants for potato development, and it was growing frustrated that farmers in the area still preferred growing grain crops. Grain crops didn't give as much return as potatoes.

So, in 1996, SaskWater, the agency that ran the dam and irrigation system, initiated a bolder approach.

First, it grew some potatoes on the irrigated land to prove they would make good french fries. The first crop of taters, that fall, went for testing to food giant Lamb Weston. The 1.7 million pounds of Saskatchewan potatoes turned black when they were fried. Not Cajun-style black, just rotten black.

Despite that first setback, SaskWater and the province decided that large-scale potato production and processing would be part of the fuel that drove Saskatchewan's development.

The goals were impressive: $120 million in investment, mostly from private investors; 730 direct jobs; 2,790 secondary jobs created; a fresh potato packing plant; and a french fry plant that would serve the world. The french fry plant would produce 300 million pounds of fries, bringing in $150 million each year.

The two thousand acres of potatoes grown in the Lake Diefenbaker area would grow to twenty thousand.

Perhaps it was a lack of imagination. Perhaps it was because the potato is such a basic food. Whatever the reason, the province gave its vision the pedestrian name of the Lake Diefenbaker Agri-Valu Strategy. Premier Roy Romanow couldn't even put the extra *e* on *Valu*. It made the whole thing seem like a discount grocery store.

SaskWater got into the act, creating its own company to oversee the potato storage and production.

Sparing no effort, the board managed to cram several words together to come up with an incredibly Canadian, all-purpose, Stompin' Tom Connors kind of name. The company would be called the Saskatchewan Potato Utility Development Company. Or Spudco.

Things were just cooking along by April 1997. The province had encouraged farmers and investors to plant potatoes for the fall harvest. That meant some new storage sheds had to go up. Spudco offered to pay 49 percent of the cost of building the $7.5-million potato storage sheds. Because there was a bit of rush, harvest being only months away, the province did not put the project out to tender. One company got the deal but refused to pay the other 51 percent. Spudco was left paying for the whole thing.

This is when things got a little tricky. Another company that wanted to build the storage sheds approached the province. Our company could have built the storage facilities for less, said the company.

In his reply, a cabinet minister reassured the company owner that Spudco, and therefore the province, was only a "minority partner" in the storage facilities. Hmm, 100 percent equals a minority?

That little slip was to cost the province a lot of money in lawsuits later on.

Meanwhile, things were looking tasty on the tater front. In January 1998, Premier Roy Romanow announced a $10-million deal between Spudco and a Chilean potato processing plant. Then Chile bailed out. Then Lamb Weston decided to build a french fry plant, not in Saskatchewan, but in Alberta. Then potato prices dropped. Meanwhile, the province received a report that Spudco had invested more than anyone thought, meaning it was in deeper water than anyone thought.

That fall, the province got more bad news. It had encouraged investors and farmers to jump aboard the potato truck, so a group calling itself the Lake Diefenbaker Potato Corporation had done just that.

By the fall of 1998, that corporation was in financial trouble. SaskWater jumped to help, sinking some taxpayers' money into the company. It didn't help. The next May, the corporation folded, owing $35 million to creditors.

By November 1999, Spudco itself was in trouble, and SaskWater asked the province for $17.8 million to bail it out. The province refused, and the next year Spudco folded.

Then they gave mail carriers Rollerblades

Back in the days when it was one of the few forms of communication available, people always complained about how slow the postal service was.

In Vancouver, they decided to do something about it. When the new central post office there opened on March 14, 1958, there was a heliport on the roof. For the helicopter. To deliver mail. This might partially explain the $13-million price tag.

The helicopter was supposed to take the mail to the train station. It was used twice. Apparently only then did people realize how expensive it was to deliver mail by helicopter.

There was also a conveyor belt in a tunnel connecting the post office to a CPR railway station that once sat at Cordova Street. It whisked mail and packages from one point to the other in under nine minutes. It cost hundreds of thousands of dollars.

The post office stopped using it by 1965, realizing that it was faster to send mail by trucks and planes, rather than trains.

The provincial auditor general released a report that said SaskWater never did figure out how it was going to get a fresh pack and french fry plant in Saskatchewan. SaskWater did not take a clear look at the potato industry itself and fully figure all the possible disasters, such as prices dropping. Nor did it do a good job telling the public or even, in some instances, the government what was going on.

By the time all the dollars had been counted, Spudco lost $27.8 million on its potato plans.

And counting. In 2000, several investors — including those in the Lake Diefenbaker Potato Corporation — sued the province for leading them down the potato garden path with promises of potato riches. They claimed losses and damages at about $100 million.

The province filed a defence, which denied having much to do with Spudco and told the investors they should have been smarter than to trust everything a provincial agency said.

But the province finally admitted in 2003 that it might have, just slightly, given the wrong impression about its involvement in the whole storage shed plan. The comments way back from the cabinet minister that the province was a minority partner assuming no risks in a private enterprise were "less than forthcoming."

The lawsuit was finally settled in 2004. The province and SaskWater paid the investors $7.9 million.

"Government had good intentions when we became involved in the construction of storage sheds," said the minister responsible for SaskWater, Peter Prebble, adding in a classic understatement, "but we made some mistakes."

A deal is a deal

Toronto is a world-class city.

Ask any city politician.

And now it's had its own world-class scandal that includes all the usual stuff of scandal — sex, abuse of power, stupidity, cupidity, and money — and, in a uniquely Canadian twist, a professional hockey player.

According to Justice Denise Bellamy, who was appointed to probe the scandal, what should have been a routine and even boring computer leasing contract ballooned into a complicated tale of greed, mismanagement, and lying.

The so-called Toronto computer leasing scandal ended up costing the city over $100 million. The biggest cost was the contract between the City of Toronto and MFP Financial Services for $40 million in computers and computer services. The city ended up spending more than $80 million under that contract.

How?

Well, to figure out that (and other aspects of the scandal) the city spent more than $19 million for a three-year inquiry, with witnesses including the treasurer, city budget chief, and a famous hockey player's brother who worked for MFP. (The hockey player made an appearance at the inquiry to testify on his brother's behalf.)

Justice Bellamy, who presided over the inquiry, said, "Some people disgraced themselves, failed in their duty to their City, lied, put self-interest first, or simply did not do their jobs." The report contains more than 240 recommendations for preventing a repeat of the scandal.

Although MFP was not the only city supplier that seemed to cross conflict-of-interest lines, its name is the one most associated with the scandal, primarily because of its leasing contract with the city — a contract that didn't have guaranteed lease rates and to which additional equipment was allowed to be added without proper approvals, some of the key reasons for the doubling of the price.

Since the beginning of the inquiry MFP has changed its name to Clearlink Capital Corp. By the summer of 2005, it had settled a number of lawsuits with other municipalities in the province.

During the inquiry Toronto decided it would not pay MFP any more money under its contract. But the city relented. In the fall of 2005, Toronto city lawyers recommended a further $9-million-plus payout to MFP to settle its claims. After all, they had a contract.

Another Toronto scandal that could cost dozens of dollars

In July 2001, when Toronto lost its bid for the 2008 Summer Olympics, distraught city leaders wrung their hands and pointed their fingers.

Mayor Mel Lastman was the target of most of the finger pointing. Only a month earlier, before visiting Kenya to promote Canada's bid to the International Olympic Committee, Lastman noted, "I'm sort of scared about going there…. I just see myself in a pot of boiling water with all these natives dancing around me."

Many IOC members were shocked, especially those from Africa. Instantly, Canada had a worse human rights reputation than China, which is not an easy feat to accomplish. Lastman had helped cannibalize his own city's bid. Beijing got the Olympics.

It wasn't the first time bizarre incidents contributed to Toronto's losing an Olympic bid. The city also failed to get the 1960 Summer Olympics.

City officials apparently lost the bid because they misplaced some paperwork. An official IOC application had been sent to the city in 1954. But no one filled it out. And no one could figure out where it had gone.

These days Olympic bids are fought and awarded with much front page hoopla. But when Toronto lost the 1960 bid, the news made it to page 28 of the *Toronto Star* on April 15, 1955. The story was not based on an announcement or even a press release. It was based on a letter from Harry Price, chairperson of the Canadian National Exhibition, to the city's Civic Parks Committee. The Civic Parks Committee, not the mayor and a thousand others, was handling the Olympic bid. The letter from Price described a phone call he had just received from Sidney Dawes, the official Canadian representative on the IOC. According to Price, Dawes told him Toronto had lost the bid.

But Dawes had some good advice for future bids: always accompany the bids with a little gift for IOC members. Over the years, Dawes said, he had collected some very nice gifts from cities competing for the Olympics.

Four decades later, a scandal erupted over the awarding of gifts to IOC members by the organizers of the 2002 Salt Lake City Olympics.

IOC members were offered cash and scholarships, trips to Disney and Las Vegas, and tickets for the Superbowl.

But this story was taking place in 1955, and the gifts back then were more understated. It's always a "very nice gesture," Dawes advised the Toronto bidders, to send each IOC member a lighter with the city crest on it.

West vs. East. We all lose.

In a contest over where governments have wasted the most money on badly run projects, it'd be a tough race between Alberta and the Atlantic provinces.

In Atlantic Canada, according to a 1995 government report, taxpayers lost $100 million between 1985 and 1992 on seventeen projects that collapsed after getting federal loans and help.

In Alberta, however, the province lost $2.3 billion on twenty-two projects from 1980 to 1994, according to the Canadian Taxpayer Federation's Mike Milke in his book *Tax Me I'm Canadian*. They do things big out west.

It's still tough to choose a winner. Although Alberta wasted more money, at least the losses were limited to provincial taxpayers' cash.

In Atlantic Canada, federal dollars went to the firms through the Atlantic Canada Opportunities Agency. In the 1995 study, auditors for the agency sang the same sad song auditors always sing after poring through government funding records. Someone came knocking on the government's door. Here's a good idea, the individual said. Lend us some money. The government didn't bother to do much checking. It just went and got its wallet and gave the person at the door some money. And kissed it goodbye.

According to the audit, the federal agency gave a cedar fencing mill in New Brunswick $850,000 after the company submitted a financial plan that predicted its own demise. The plan was accurate. The company lasted one whole year.

The seventeen companies referred to in the 1995 report ranged from a resort in Newfoundland to an aerospace company in Nova Scotia.

The report was a secret, but Canadian Press dug it up and newspapers across the country repeated the story. Canadians were outraged.

And in the years following, nothing much changed.

Take Polar Foods, for example. Or as residents of Prince Edward Island would joke, Take Polar Foods, please.

Seafood processing is an important industry in P.E.I., employing about 2,500 people in 1997. Throughout the seventies and early eighties, the province put a lot of money into increasing the processing of seafood, even as the federal government was starting to limit the harvest of seafood. That made it harder for lobster processors to make good money. In 1997 the province took a look at the problem and discovered that all the lobster processing plants were working at only 22 percent capacity during the lobster season. Nonetheless, the next year, nine lobster processing companies amalgamated under a new name, Polar Foods, and convinced the province to invest $7 million and guarantee a loan of $7.5 million a year for five years.

The province didn't bother to check the financial statements of the nine companies to see how they were doing. That might have been a good idea. Only a year after the merger, Polar Foods came back to the province for more money. And kept coming back. One of the big problems was the fact that the lobster processing market hadn't improved just because nine companies were run under one name. As losses mounted each year, the province still failed to properly monitor Polar Foods.

The details of the collapse are contained in fifty pages of the P.E.I. auditor general's report released in 2005. Suffice it to say that by the time Polar Foods went under in 2004, P.E.I. taxpayers had lost $31 million. It was the largest amount lost to a single enterprise yet.

The good people of P.E.I. shouldn't feel too bad. They've got lots of company down east.

In 2001, NB Power began planning to convert an oil generating station in Coleson Cove, New Brunswick, to a plant that burned Orimulsion. Orimulsion is a low-cost, heavy fossil fuel produced only in Venezuela. The conversion would cost $700 million, but NB Power said the fuel would produce less pollution and the loan for the conversion would be paid off within six years of completion, around 2011. NB Power would not reveal the price it was going to pay for Orimulsion because the contract was confidential. There is an agreement in principle, NB Power said.

The utility company went ahead with its refit of the Coleson Cove plant, even though there was the minor detail that the deal wasn't signed. Then something went wrong. Venezuela refused to provide the special fuel. In 2004, NB Power launched a $2-billion lawsuit against the Venezuelan companies that produce the fuel. At the same time, several NB Power officials resigned. In early 2005, the mess was handed to the provincial auditor general. By the end of the year, no report had been issued, but it was already clear that Coleson Cove could be added to the list of Atlantic Canada bungles.

Alberta's collection of troubled projects is equally impressive, ranging from a $646-million loss on Novatel computer systems to a mere $2 million on a recreation products company.

Of special note is the saga of the Swan Hills hazardous waste management facility, which combined financial waste with environmental hazards in its draining of $440 million in taxpayers' money.

The Swan Hills saga began in 1982, when Bovar Inc. was chosen to build a hazardous waste treatment facility in Swan Hills. Five years later, the government-owned Alberta Special Waste Management Corporation signed a deal with Bovar, guaranteeing it a minimum rate of return of prime plus 3 percent for the next ten years, even if the plant lost money. In 1992, Alberta, under the leadership of then Environment Minister Ralph Klein, approved a $104-million expansion of the Swan Hills facility in order to handle oil field waste. Any day now, Klein figured, oil field waste was going to be classified as hazardous. A year later, the Environmental Protection Act was passed, excluding oil field waste as hazardous material. That little error in judgement costs the province $500,000.

Still, the province decided Swan Hills was working out all right. In one strange agreement, the province sold its 40 percent share to Bovar but ended up paying Bovar $147 million to run the plant for the next three years.

With the financial hazards firmly in place, the Swan Hills facility embarked on a series of environmental hazards. Dioxins, furans, and PCBs leaked out of the plant in October 1996, and two months later Alberta Health warned residents to eat limited amounts of game and fish in a thirty-kilometre radius around the plant. The next year, an explosion released more PCBs, dioxins, and furans into the air. Things got so bad that the federal government stopped sending waste there. The news just got worse. A federal study in 1998 showed aboriginals who lived near the plant had higher PCB levels than average.

With all the bad press, Bovar was having trouble making money. It started layoffs in 1999, was refused a government bailout in 2000, and promptly shut down.

The province tried to sell the plant but got no takers. For the next three years it cost the province about $15 million a year to operate. Finally, in 2003, the province agreed to pay a private company to operate the facility. The cost to the government, $1 million a year and — you'd think they'd learn — a share in any losses.

A failure in progress

Sometimes modern history just gives everyone a headache.

In 1995, Quebec held a referendum that could have led to separation.

The question itself was a portent of the mess to come: "Do you agree that Quebec should become sovereign, after having made a formal offer to Canada for a new economic and political partnership, within the scope of the bill respecting the future of Quebec and of the agreement signed on June 12, 1995?"

Voting "no" meant voting "yes" to Canada.

After the Liberal government of Prime Minister Jean Chrétien failed to take the threat seriously, busloads of ordinary Canadians raced to Montreal for a giant rally that may have turned the tide and persuaded a slim majority of Quebecers to vote "no."

(Quebec Premier Jacques Parizeau blamed the loss on "money and the ethnic vote." He did not mean the Canadians on the buses.)

Scared by the near loss, the Liberals set up a program to promote national unity.

They spent $250 million. Most of the money went into Quebec. Much of it went into Quebec via advertising companies that were hooked up with the Liberals. With much of the money, the ad firms did nothing or next to nothing. Some of the money went to the ad firms and then back to the Liberal party. This is called a kickback.

When the Canadian public figured out what was going on, it got downright perturbed. Quebec was especially angry. The Liberals were not only condescending by trying to buy loyalty but also cheats.

So by 2004 the separatist movement in Quebec got a boost by the very millions of dollars that were supposed to quell it.

A federal election was called, and the 2005–06 election campaign began. Only school years and hockey seasons should extend over two years.

No Canada-wide party could win a majority.

In fact, no Canada-wide party existed. The Conservatives kept their stranglehold on the West, which hated the Liberals, and made small inroads into Ontario and Quebec. Liberal support remained strong in the Maritimes and in Ontario, which also hated the Liberals but couldn't stomach the Conservatives. The NDP got the usual handful of seats here and there. The Bloc Quebecois, of course, took Quebec, but its support fell in the only province that really cares.

Ten years and $250 million in unity funding, and the country was in greater disunity than ever.

Now that's failure.

CHAPTER 9

INVENTIONS

Canadians are inventive at making things, just not necessarily the right things. And if they do manage to make the right things, they just aren't good at making money from them.

The carrot, Canada's medical miracle

If Canada had embraced the ideas of visionary George L. Kavanagh, we'd have twice as many uses for carrots as we do now. We'd have to be a lot more careful when making stew, though.

Thinking way, way outside the box, Kavanagh filed a patent in 1926 for an unusual treatment for certain diseases.

"This invention relates to improvements in [the] method of treating certain diseases, especially rectal diseases and the object of the invention is to provide a safe, convenient and not uncomfortable method of treating the primary cause of such diseases," Kavanagh wrote.

"It has been determined that the primary cause of many rectal and intestinal diseases is constipation and, according to this invention, the various diseases are treated primarily by removing their initial cause."

In some detail, he describes how the "soft, pliable and highly elastic" internal and external sphincters of youth shrink and lose their elasticity as one ages. Thus the anus and rectum contract.

"This gradual reduction of orifice area combined with the gradually reducing activity of advancing age results in a gradually increasing retention of waste products."

Lubricants and medicine provide only temporary comfort. Kavanagh came up with a longer-lasting treatment.

"The treatment is effected by gently dilating the anus and rectum until the organs are restored to their youthful size. This dilation is of course mechanical, but is assisted to a certain extent by the application of suitable medicinal preparations."

The best dilators, Kavanagh reasoned, would be inexpensive and easily obtained. Ideally, the size of the dilator could be increased as treatment continues. The perfect dilator, then — the common carrot.

"An ordinary carrot is shaped by means of a suitable instrument into a cylindrical body of suitable size having a blunt point and an enlarged butt end. This serves as both an applicator for medicinal preparations and as a dilator," Kavanagh proposed.

How to put the medicine in? Simple. Just carve a recess in the carrot for a capsule of the desired medicinal preparation. One could carve the recess in the appropriate spot of the carrot, depending on exactly where the preparation was to be applied.

Think about it, Kavanagh urged. "The applicator is preferably dipped in boiling water immediately before use for the purpose of softening the outer surface of the vegetable matter and converting the same to a species of lubricant."

Aha, carrot juice. And in the boiling water could be dissolved any medical preparations needed.

The applicator would be held in place by a "suitable form of harness," presumably not the human hand.

"The applicator is renewed as often as necessary and, at the discretion of the physician supervising the treatment, applicators of gradually increasing size are used. After a reasonable length of time a permanently enlarged condition of the organs results, which is merely the restoration to their normal condition."

One could use other vegetable matter, Kavanagh suggests, but other legumes would serve only a mechanical purpose. "The carrot is chosen on account of its recognized soothing and healing effect when applied in the form of a poultice to inflamed surfaces," he determined.

The applications were numerous, and Kavanagh wasn't taking any chances of others butting in on his idea. It could treat stomach, intestinal, and rectal diseases, he noted.

No one knows what happened to Kavanagh's carrot dilator. It appears we Canadians, over the years, put it politely but firmly behind us.

Ben Franklin, he isn't

Hey, when you come up with literally hundreds of ideas for inventions, not all of them are going to be great. Take Alexander Graham Bell, for example.

Bell, as most of us know, is famous for his telephone invention. He came up with lots of other ideas, too. But even geniuses have bad days and bad ideas.

Like the Cygnet II — a plane made with wings created from a wall of kites.

Bell had been playing around with tetrahedral kites. And apparently he thought that a nice wall of tetrahedral kites would be just the thing to get a plane off the ground.

So he had a half-ton of kites built. That's 3,960 tetrahedral kites constructed and then fastened together into a wall. These were the wings. He hung a fuselage and motor off the whole shebang and voila — a flying wall of fun.

Bell was sixty-two when this little wonder was put together at Badeck, Nova Scotia, so he didn't actually try to pilot this contraption. A young man by the name of J.A.D. McCurdy had that honour on February 22, 1909.

Now, let's just review.

Aeronautically speaking, for something to get off the ground, there has to be lift. That's what a wing does. Kites can fly because they are wings and the wind can lift them off the ground. And Bell had conducted an experiment where a big triangle of tetrahedral kites provided powerful lift.

So a wing made of tetrahedral kites should provide lots of lift, right? Well, yes.

But in 1909 there was no engine in the world that could push almost four thousand kites through the air fast enough to get the contraption airborne. That's because the resistance of the wall of kites was greater than the lift.

It was an important lesson in aeronautics. Fortunately everyone got to walk away from this tutorial, mostly because the experiment, conducted on a frozen lake, the perfect natural airfield, was such a failure. Riding the wall of kites, McCurdy sort of swanned around the frozen lake surface until it was pretty clear the Cygnet was a dodo.

What does this guy have to do to get noticed?

When you think radio, you probably think Guglielmo Marconi.

And you probably think Canada's role in the invention of the radio was to provide some real estate for the first intercontinental radio broadcast.

You'd be wrong.

First, the broadcast was made in Newfoundland long before it ever entered Confederation. And second, don't think Marconi. Think Fessenden.

Reginald Fessenden was a Quebec-born inventor who, like many Canadian inventors, may have been a genius but could have used some help with marketing and publicity.

When Fessenden was growing up in Ontario, his uncle, a physics teacher, brought him to see Alexander Graham Bell in 1876, the year Bell invented the telephone. Fessenden liked the telephone but was curious about why it required wires to connect the two sets. Right then and there, Fessenden decided he was going to broadcast voices through the air.

And he did. Before Marconi.

In 1901, Marconi managed to send a radio signal across the Atlantic with the message in the dots and dashes of Morse code. Marconi had a theory of why this happened, but it was wrong and Fessenden knew it. He recognized that a radio, to be useful, would need to use a standing wave; that is, it would have to broadcast continuously, not in little spurts of sparks as his contemporaries believed. Fessenden's first speech broadcast was looked on with something like amusement — why use speech when you can spark off some dots and dashes? And other scientists ridiculed his theories of the continuous wave.

Fessenden's first speech broadcast took place on December 23, 1900 — the year before Marconi's trans-Atlantic transmission of dots and dashes. He transmitted his own voice over the first wireless telephone from a site on Cobb Island in the middle of the Potomac River near Washington, D.C.

In 1906, with Marconi still playing about with sparks and arcs and dots and dashes, Fessenden broadcast music and speech to ships in the Atlantic. In 1906 he also managed two-way voice communication between Scotland and Massachusetts.

Instead of getting rich, his backers seized his patents and pushed him aside. He sued. That took almost two decades to settle. When all was said and done, he won about $500,000 in damages and handed over about $300,000 in lawyers' fees.

He wound up working in the United States building radios for that country's military. In Canada, he couldn't get the funding to do research.

And when he tried to create a radio network in Canada, he was told he couldn't. The Canadian government had given that privilege exclusively to Marconi — who was not a Canadian.

In 1929 Fessenden invented a television. He also developed a kind of sonar to help the world avoid another *Titanic* disaster by helping ships detect icebergs. The same invention came in handy during the First World War, helping ships detect submarines.

During that war, he also created a device that would allow the Canadian military to detect enemy artillery and determine its range and location. His sense of patriotism had brought him back to Canada and he was sent to work on the device in London, England. But the bureaucrats who approved purchases for the military weren't interested. (A Canadian army officer later created a similar device out of necessity, at the front, driven by the horrific losses of men to German artillery.)

In all, Fessenden was a holder of more than five hundred patents. He was highly regarded in the United States. He was awarded money and recognition by the city of Philadelphia as "one whose labors have been of great benefit to mankind." The Institute of Radio Engineers of America presented him with its medal of honour. The head of General Electric Laboratories called him "the greatest wireless inventor of the age — greater than Marconi."

The *New York Times* wrote an editorial regarding Fessenden:

> It sometimes happens, even in science, that one man can be right against the world. Professor Fessenden was that man. He fought bitterly and alone to prove his theories. It was he who insisted, against the stormy protests of every recognized authority, that what we now call radio was worked by continuous waves sent through the ether by the transmitting station as light waves are sent out by a flame. Marconi and others insisted that what was happening was a whiplash effect. The progress of radio was retarded a decade by this error. The whiplash theory passed gradually from the minds of men and was replaced by the continuous wave — one with all too little credit to the man who had been right.

Prior to his death, Fessenden wrote:

> In my lifetime, I developed over a hundred patentable inventions including the electric gyroscope, the hetero-dyne, and a depth finder. I built the first power generating station at Niagara Falls and I invented radio, sending the first wireless voice message in the world on Dec. 23, 1900.
>
> But despite all my hard work, I lived most of my life near poverty. I fought years of court battles before seeing even a penny from my greatest inventions. And worst of all, I was ridiculed by journalists, businessmen, and even other scientists, for believing that voice could ever be transmitted without using wires. But by the time death was near, not only was I wealthy from my patents, and all of those people who had laughed at my ideas were twisting the dials on their newly bought radios to hear the latest weather and news.

In many American encyclopedia and reference books, he is considered a Canadian American, even though he never gave up his Canadian citizenship and when war was declared he returned to Canada to serve, although his genius had been ignored and gone unrewarded in his own country.

Even today the *Encyclopedia Canadiana* does not give him a separate listing. Mention of him is included only under the listing for his mother, Clementina, who established Empire Day in Canada. Reginald is mentioned as one of her four sons, "inventor of the wireless telephone, the radio compass and the visible bullet for machine guns, he also invented the first television set in North America in 1919."

Still — no credit for the radio.

Another great Canadian idea, another great U.S. success story

That Thomas Edison — a great guy. He invented the light bulb and changed the way the world ... um, not really.

It's sad but true. Two men from Toronto, Henry Woodward and Matthew Evans, invented a light bulb *before* Edison. But they couldn't get the financing they needed to get their invention from the lab to the store windows. So they sold the rights to their 1875 patent to Edison. In 1879, Edison demonstrated his light globe — one of the inventions most associated with his name. Like so many other great Canadian ideas, Woodward and Evans's invention ended up going south.

Instant camera, instant anonymity

On the weekend, you probably like to head off into the country for a picnic with your friends and family and take a few photographs with the McCurdy and ...

What, you've never heard of a McCurdy?

Well you would have, had Arthur Williams McCurdy been as much businessman as inventor.

McCurdy was a genius when it came to inventions. One of them was a method of making pictures anywhere — not just taking them but *making* them. It was called the Portable Film Developing System, and McCurdy created it in 1890. A little ahead of his time.

Even so, thirteen years later, when the world caught up to him, he sold the patent to George Eastman. Yes, as in Eastman Kodak Co. It took decades for the first Polaroid cameras to come onto the market. And McCurdy was long forgotten.

Invent the converter first, then I'll buy more channels

Long before pay television and satellite service, long before even cable, the movie company Famous Players came up with the idea that viewers might want to make their own selections of shows each night. The company developed the Telemeter and decided to test it in Etobicoke, Ontario, in 1960.

For a mere five-dollar installation fee, residents would get the coin-operated Telemeter decoding box installed.

Then, simply by dropping in one dollar in coins, they could watch movies on Channels A or B. Newscasts were provided free on Channel C.

You'd think most of the 150,000 residents living in Etobicoke at the time would have rushed out to get a Telemeter. Their other choices were one Toronto station, one Hamilton station, and — if they were lucky and the weather over Lake Ontario was clear — two Buffalo stations.

Life was simpler then. Television in the home was still a new thing and people must have been happy just to have two channels. Maybe they still read those things called books. Only five thousand households signed up for the service, which started February 26, 1960. Famous Players hung on to the idea for five years, then pulled the plug. There just wasn't the demand for pay television yet.

Making waves but not money

It took almost ten years, but in 1936 the young inventor Morse Robb stood poised to ride a wave that would crash over the musical world and take it by storm. His wave. His wave organ.

Robb had invented the new kind of organ back in 1927 in his family home in Belleville, Ontario. At the time, inventors and manufacturers across the world were trying to replicate the sound pipe organs make so the ordinary consumer could have something in their home that made the parlour sound like church, without the huge pipes and huge costs.

Some tried radio tubes electronics, the approach that led to the development of today's house organs. Robb had a different idea. He wanted to record the actual waveform of a pipe organ and then recreate it electrically. He had each pipe from the organ at the Bridge Street United Church in Belleville sounded, and he recorded each tone on an oscillograph. Then he photographed each waveform. These pictures he used to trace out and cut steel discs. When the steel discs were spun near an electromagnetic head, they produced electric impulses. Run through an amplifier, the impulses made the sound of the original tone of the pipe organ.

It was complicated, but it worked. For the next three years, Robb took his wave organ prototype to musicians, manufacturers, and music critics. Everyone was impressed. In 1927, just when he could have signed with a manufacturer, Robb decided to patent the organ and manufacture it on his own. It was a bad idea. Getting the patent cost a lot of money, and in 1929 the Great Depression hit. No one had much money to develop a new kind of organ.

But Robb pushed on, getting money here and money there, until in 1934 he was able to set up the Robb Wave Organ Company in Belleville. He sold a few of the organs in 1936 to stores and chapels. One was demonstrated at the Canadian National Exhibition in 1937.

But Robb was doomed before he even got started. Few people had the money to buy his $2,000 to $2,600 models of the wave organ. Few people made that in a year.

Sales suffered, and after all his work Robb suffered a nervous breakdown. In 1939, Hammond introduced its electronic organ, and eleven years later it introduced its first simple chord organ, easy to play and costing about $1,000. Hammond became the household name in organs. Robb eventually recovered and got a job in manufacturing. Not organs.

CHAPTER 10

ODDS AND
ODD ENDINGS

These stories failed to make it elsewhere in the book. Does that make them success stories? Not likely.

Ever get that sinking feeling?

Any kid in a sandbox or on a beach knows you can't dig too many tunnels underneath a sand castle or the whole thing will collapse.

Life is never that simple outside the sandbox, though.

Imagine the same castle and the same tunnels in the adult world. The people who own the castle don't own the land beneath. The people who own the land beneath really want to dig tunnels and really don't care too much about what happens to the castles.

That sums up Edmonton's Riverdale neighbourhood in the twenties and thirties. Seams of coal ran out to the North Saskatchewan River, which runs through the city, and as far back as 1879 coal mines tapped those seams.

Just about any enterprising fellow could open up a mine. For $10 to $20 an acre, depending on the quality of coal, you could buy the mineral rights to up to 320 acres.

It was a nice arrangement. One person could dig underneath while letting someone else build a house or school or neighbourhood on top.

Mining companies came and went, but by the twenties, three outfits had wormed their way underneath Riverdale to tap one particularly large coal seam. A few city officials began warning politicians that perhaps building tunnels under a neighbourhood wasn't a good idea. They also warned politicians that the new sewage disposal plant was sitting too close to the coal tunnels. Sure enough, the ground under one sewage tank cracked and sewage leaked into the river.

Everyone started to sound warnings: the school board, residents, sports leagues. People complained not only of noise from mining underneath their houses and shocks from underground blasts but also of cracking, creeping foundations.

The city did a study in 1926. No action was taken, but the city did start asking the province for help. Because the mineral rights were held by private companies, the city needed provincial legislation to stop the mining.

The province considered. More homes cracked and shifted. The province continued to consider.

City of Edmonton Archives, EA-75-351

The Archer family in Edmonton almost learned the hard way that coal mines shouldn't be dug under residential neighbourhoods. When brothers Calvin and Vernon tried to light the coal furnace one cold February morning, the room exploded.

One of the considerations was just how valuable coal was to the city's economy. About 100,000 tons of coal worth about $300,000 were being produced each year. In 1925, two mines in Riverdale paid more than $176,000 in workers' wages.

Then, on January 22, 1930, the area started to get a really big sinking feeling.

"To awaken from a sound sleep at 3 a.m. and feel the house sinking was the unique and somewhat terrifying feeling of a family living in Rowland Road," reported that day's *Edmonton Journal*.

Under the page 13 headline "Family Awakens at 3 a.m. to find House Sinking," the *Journal* described the scene. "As you walk along the floors now you can feel them all uneven and heaving as you proceed. Outside there are great cracks in the walls and the sills have been torn away from the windows to the extent you could drop a cat in."

Only days later, another house had to be evacuated after two walls cracked so much they were liable to collapse.

A month after that, twenty-one-year-old Calvin Archer and his eighteen-year-old brother, Vernon, went into the family basement to light the coal fire furnace. Calvin struck a match against the side of the furnace and, boom, just like that, the room exploded. Calvin and Vernon flew across the room. The blast broke every window in the house, destroyed a main-floor kitchen wall, and knocked the entire house off its moorings. Mrs. Archer and three other children were in the kitchen and were thrown to the floor. Although Calvin suffered burns to his face and hands, no one was killed. But they were mighty upset. It turned out a gas main thirty-five feet away had broken and the gas had seeped into the basement. The cause of the leak? The sinking of the ground because of the coal mines.

Meanwhile, the city engineer who had first sounded the alarm sounded some more. James Church declared a neighbourhood school unsafe because the bank it was built on was in danger of sliding away.

Penn Coal fought back. In a quarter-page ad on March 1 in the *Edmonton Journal*, the company pointed out it had paid $264,664 in salary in the past year. The figures "convey to the citizens of Edmonton the importance of the industry in our community."

But the advertising could do only so much. Another city report, this time in 1930, painted a picture of mines zigzagging underneath all of Riverdale, with some zigs and zags quite large.

With houses crumbling, reports piling up, and public opinion shifting, the province finally created a law to stop Penn Mine from digging.

Then the fight over compensation began. Owners of 115 properties submitted claims, but that number jumped up when the province announced $12,000 would be split up among the deserving. The catch of the province's gift was that the city could make no further claims on provincial money.

It wasn't nearly enough money, and it took two years for the city to hand it out.

Meanwhile, the neighbourhood kept sinking. On May 20, 1935, the *Edmonton Journal* reported that the front yard of a home "collapsed with a dull roar." The hole, about six metres in diameter and about four metres deep, was only a step away from the front of the house.

That was the last near-disaster, but even today, residents say the ground occasionally shifts. Golfers at the Riverside golf course, built over the site of one large mine, complain that the way the greens break changes every year. It's the shifting ground, the golfers claim, not shifting skills.

Who was supposed to fill the salt tunnels back up?

At first, workers thought little of the rumbling sound.

"I felt a jolt and heard a rumble and the thought crossed my mind that they might have begun blasting on the new salt mine," said Jim Allan, a yard foreman at the Canadian Industries Limited plant in Windsor, Ontario. The plant manufactured chlorine from the salt mined next door by Canadian Salt Company.

"I thought it was just freight trains shunting in the yard," said H.R. Bishop, the plant fire chief.

A few minutes later, at about 9:30 a.m. on February 19, 1954, Allan was called to a pump room to help fix a broken pipe. At first it was just one pipe, then another and another began to leak. A fire alarm sounded and Bishop rushed to the room. Steam and water was leaking everywhere. A road outside the plant began to sag and water seeped over it. By then, the workers knew this was no ordinary rumbling.

Shortly after noon, the centre of the seventy-five-acre plant started to sink. Metre-high water spouts shot into the air from the ground. Muddy waves rolled across sinking buildings.

A Canadian Salt official decided to walk over on the connecting spur line to help out. When the tracks started to sink, he changed his mind.

By 3:30 p.m., three separate buildings had sunk seven metres into the ground and were covered with a pond about one hundred metres wide. "They were like little boats going down in a sea of mud," said one witness.

No one was hurt and soon the 300 workers were sent home. So were about 150 workers at the nearby Canadian Salt Company when its parking lot began to settle.

The next morning work crews surveyed the damage. Two buildings used to pump and liquefy chlorine gas and a washroom were partially submerged. A large warehouse owned by Canadian Salt was almost completely underwater. Rail lines were buckled. Chlorine gas was leaking from a storage tank and there was the smell of sewage, probably from

Tourists just don't care about electric clocks

The world's first steam-powered clock can still be seen in Gastown, in downtown Vancouver, British Columbia.

Every fifteen minutes it whistles and steam shoots out, causing delight among groups of tourists gathered around it. It's said to be one of the most photographed sites in Vancouver.

But the clock doesn't actually run on steam. It runs on electricity.

It did run on steam for a short, but chronologically chaotic, period. Hard to say how long, really, because it didn't work.

It was a notoriously bad timepiece when it did run on steam. A clock really needs only a tiny coiled spring to make it run. And steam is powerful stuff — it powers locomotives and electric generators. This makes it tough to regulate in a manner necessary for good timekeeping. A steam clock could run through an hour in twenty seconds.

That's why steam clocks never caught on. And why this one is such a tourist attraction.

This clock does keep pretty good time now that it's an electric clock with steam "enhancements." Most guidebooks, however, still promote it as a working steam clock.

broken lines, in the air. A little shed bobbed in the water like a boat, about fifty metres from where it had stood the day before. Scaffolding supporting chlorine lines had toppled down.

It took weeks to clean up the mess and get the plant operating again, with CIL figuring it lost about $1 million in damages and lost production.

The history of salt was to blame. The cave-in occurred where original salt mines were dug in 1905, about 350 metres below the surface. Over the years, wells had been sunk and water had been forced into salt veins, then pumped again as brine. Geologists brought in to examine the damage said a shift in the rock 350 metres below might have filled in some of the old wells, forcing the water up. When the ground settled, so did the plant.

That's why all his maps are upside down

Samuel de Champlain is considered by many people to be the father of Canada, so it's not surprising that we try to keep him on a bit of a pedestal. Literally. There are statues of him dotted across the country, including one in our nation's capital.

The historical basis for that statue is, to say the least, a bit murky. Not far from Ottawa is a place called Cobden's Green Lake, where early travellers in Canada used to portage around a nasty piece of rapids. Champlain wrote in his diary about taking this route around the rapids. (He also complained in his diary about all the things he had to carry on his own — so much for the myth about early explorers stoically roughing it in the bush.)

Skip ahead a few hundred years — 254 to be exact. It was the summer of 1867, appropriately enough, the year of Confederation. Fourteen-year-old Edward Lee was helping his father clear some forest in the area of the old portage, near Cobden's Green Lake, in eastern Ontario. Under an old log, he found some old cups and an astrolabe.

One story has it that Edward's father gave the astrolabe to his boss, Richard Cassels of Toronto. Cassels was president of the Union Forwarding and Railway Company of Ottawa. Apparently Edward was supposed to receive the equivalent of ten dollars or so but never got his cash.

(Another version of the story is that a riverboat captain who worked for Cassels, named Cowley, promised to pay Edward ten dollars for the item and it was Cowley who gave it to Cassels, who owned the riverboat. In this version, Cassels still gets the astrolabe and Edward still doesn't get paid.)

So we know Champlain travelled this way and we know an astrolabe was found that was made at the right time for Champlain to have owned it. So it must be his, right?

Yet there was no mention of the loss in his diary. An astrolabe is not something you would want to misplace — early travellers used them to find the latitude of their location, the time of day, when an upcoming astronomical event (like an eclipse) would take place, and other information useful to someone on the go. Losing your astrolabe would likely be worthy of a mention in your diary.

Nevertheless, because two nineteenth-century newspaper reporters ran with the story that it was Champlain's astrolabe, it's been linked with him ever since.

And while even government publications say it's his, the government hasn't always been interested in actually owning it.

Cassels, who obtained the astrolabe from Edward one way or another, willed it to his son Walter. Walter apparently recognized the historic significance of the instrument. In 1897, he offered it to Quebec City, which was not interested in paying the requested $1,000 price tag. A similar offer was turned down a year or so later.

Finally, in 1901, the astrolabe was sold to a New Jersey antique collector and scholar, Samuel Hoffman. Hoffman later became president of the New York Historical Society, and when he died in 1942 he willed the astrolabe to that organization.

It stayed there until 1989. Even with federal politicians talking up the importance of the astrolabe, even with them buying into the story told by two newspapermen, they couldn't buy into the idea of buying the astrolabe. Eventually, however, they changed their minds — paying a cool quarter of a million dollars for it.

Perhaps government officials realized it was inconsistent to decline buying the astrolabe itself when they had erected a large statue to honour Champlain at Nepean Point in Ottawa. There he stands, glorious and cloaked, holding aloft the precious astrolabe — no doubt about to take some important reading or other. It's a wonderful sculpture.

Only two things wrong with it, really.

First, Champlain, one of the best mapmakers of his day, is holding his astrolabe upside down. If the sculptor, Hamilton MacCarthy, had perhaps asked his son for advice on the navigational device's orientation, he might have got it right. His son was an engineer.

The other is that the model for the sculpture wasn't actually Champlain. To be fair, there is no surviving likeness of Champlain except for a sketch, thought to be made by the man himself, of Champlain firing an arquebus during a battle with the Iroquois.

But MacCarthy used as a model a painting of a contemporary member of the French court and said it was Champlain. As it turned out, the person he picked as a model for the father of our country was a bit of a scoundrel — a fraud artist, in fact. And apparently one who didn't know how to hold an astrolabe.

Um, we said we wanted customers, but not at any cost

The year is 1909.

Vancouver medical and emergency workers are positively bursting with pride.

Why?

The city's first ambulance has arrived.

It's a wonder of modern science and technology — even though it's early in the history of the automobile. Which might suggest that particular care be taken in driving it, especially for those unfamiliar with automobiles and driving.

On its first trip in the hands of the city crew, the ambulance ran over an American tourist and killed him. This took place in front of the old Fader's grocery store at the corner of Pender and Granville.

The deceased tourist was picked up, put in the back of the ambulance, and taken to the city morgue.

No one else was run over on the way.

Try this; it's called a parachute

Look, up in the sky! It's a bird. No, no, it's much bigger than a bird! It's a plane. No, no, it's too small for a plane.

And it's kind of dark out, so it's actually hard to see what it is.

Why it must be Falling-Like-A-Brick Man.

Falling-Like-A-Brick Man — when not a superhero — was a guy who liked to jump off buildings, usually in a single bound. This is called BASE jumping.

BASE is an acronym for buildings, antennae, spans, and earth, and BASE jumping is a so-called extreme sport that has seen people leap from some of the world's tallest landmarks. Usually they try not to hit them on the way down.

But one day in April 2005, Falling-Like-A-Brick Man tried jumping off the Canada Trust building in Calgary. Everything was going very well. That is to say, he was plunging downward in a manner that was apparently according to plan.

Until the wind blew him into the side of the building, whereupon he smashed a window on the twenty-fourth floor — and his pelvis, back, and some internal organs. The broken glass joined him on his downward plunge, until he eventually landed on the domed glass ceiling of an atrium on the fifth floor, breaking several other panes of glass, said police sergeant Mike Lomore. This wasn't according to plan.

Police found him lying on the pedestrian walkway, but they had to use a helicopter to locate him. The superhero's girlfriend, who was to be his assistant in making the getaway, called the police after things went, um, sideways.

He was taken to hospital for treatment.

Who's going to watch the second last duel?

If you're a small town in Ontario and you want to get a slice of the lucrative tourist pie — that would not be a pie made out of tourists, by the way — you need a gimmick.

It's not enough to be cute and pretty and surrounded by natural beauty. And the leaders of Perth knew this. But they had the answer. What says family entertainment and fun like a good old-fashioned duel?

So Perth laid claim to the "Last Fatal Duel In Canada." It was a shoot-out between John Wilson and Robert Lyon in 1833, which Wilson won.

But according to Hugh Halliday, author of *Murder Among Gentlemen: A History of Duelling in Canada*, it was not the last fatal duel in Canada. Which he explained in his letter to Perth in 1982.

According to Halliday, the last fatal duel was the Warde-Sweeney duel of 1838.

"Since 1982 when this writer brought the Warde-Sweeney duel to Perth's attention, spokesmen for that town have endeavoured to sweep it under the rug with the dubious argument that the incident of 1838 did not constitute a proper duel. At the same time, Perth has continued to trumpet the false claim. Civic pride demands that a dubious honour be upheld and damn the facts of history," says Halliday.

No matter. Even Stompin' Tom Connors wrote a song about the Perth duel, further solidifying the claim. And in 1997 two Sheridan College film students made a film about the duel. In Perth, tourist literature, placements, and other mementos support the claim. There's even a last duel park.

Halliday has a problem with the re-enactments of duels and a warning to other towns that might try the same. Historically speaking, he says, duel re-enactments are "a tasteless gesture, celebrating what was at best a stupid display of snobbish pride and if not, a criminal act."

So there.

But we did get the island of Newfoundland

Canada may not be a tropical paradise, but it could have had one. A few times. Sadly, however, we've never quite managed it.

Let's skip back a century or so to when one of Canada's great heroes, Sir Sanford Fleming, was working on a plan for a trans-Pacific cable. The year was 1894. Fleming had been constantly encouraging and cajoling the British to take possession of an island in the mid-Pacific and lay claim to it. At the time, believe it or not, there were still plenty of small pieces of land that the Europeans and Americans hadn't yet laid claim to.

Fleming was partial to a property that was part of the Hawaiian Islands. And why not? It was perfectly placed and had no one living on it. It had been most recently discovered by the French in the 1700s and named by the French captain who found it — Necker, after France's then minister of finance. (Actually, it was a barren rock in the middle of the biggest ocean in the world with supine plant life and covered from one end to the other with birds and the stuff that comes out of birds. Kind of perfect for remembering a minister of finance of any country, really.)

Britain was sluggish, to say the least, and Fleming, worried that someone else might spot the strategic significance of Necker Island, hired a retired naval captain living in Toronto by the name of R.E.H. Gardner-Bruckner to help. Gardner-Bruckner's secret mission was to go to Hawaii, hire a steamer to take him to Necker Island, survey it, and then put up the Union Jack, laying claim to the island for the British Empire.

At the time Fleming developed his plan, Hawaii was an independent country with about forty thousand residents, governed by a queen, legislature, and cabinet. Oh, and it also had four hundred Americans who ran sugar plantations. Things were soon to change.

First, the British told the Americans what the Canadians were up to. And the Americans told the expatriates living in Hawaii. The expats were already busy plotting a coup.

They belonged to something called the Hawaiian League (named because it was in Hawaii, not because any actual Hawaiians were members). With an American warship in the harbour, the Hawaiian League threatened the Queen of Hawaii, and she stepped down as the leader of the country, believing that the United States of America would quickly reinstate her as monarch once word of the coup got out. As it turned out, the United States so liked the idea of having Hawaii as part of the good old U.S.A. that they made it a territory. And Necker was claimed as part of the Hawaiian Islands.

Fleming eventually did get Britain to claim a Pacific Island, but it was farther away and added another $2.5 million to the cost of the trans-Pacific cable.

But that's not the only time we blew a chance for a tropical paradise.

Even as far back as the 1880s, Canada's stable government and reputation for being not as bloody-minded as the Americans and British was attractive to many. Jamaica made a number of gestures of interest in a union with Canada. All to no avail.

And after the First World War, Prime Minister Robert Borden was approached by the West Indies about adding them to the Confederation. Lloyd George, Prime Minister of Great Britain, suggested Canada take over responsibility of the whole of the West Indies. Borden noted this offer in his diary but did not follow it up. Since that time, some of the West Indies have become independent. Not, of course, the British Virgin Islands, which are still a colony of Britain.

Dominica, an island northwest of Barbados, also wanted to join Canadian confederation. In the 1960s, the people of this 750-square-kilometre island with a population of eighty-five thousand thought we might be interested. But there was talk of Canada not wanting to be a colonial power. And talk of Canada needing to add to its armed forces if it took on a responsibility so far away. And so we said no.

Most recently, in 1987, Canada was approached by the Turks and Caicos Islands to be adopted into our confederation. Well, we have pretty high standards and a reputation for looking at the long view. In 1987, the Turks and Caicos was a pretty small enterprise with only ten thousand people — 90 percent of whom wanted to join Canada. We turned them down. Perhaps we were too busy worrying about our own annexation by the United States through the Free Trade Agreement.

But all may not be lost. In 2003, Peter Goldring, a member of the old Alliance Party, started up another effort to bring the Turks and Caicos into the Canadian fold. As far as Goldring (member of Parliament for Edmonton East) was concerned, the issue of the Canadian tropics hadn't cooled off.

How come no one told the oxen?

We Canadians don't like change. When change threatens, we resort to predictions of failure. When change threatens without government spending to reassure us, we get even more worried.

Take, for example, this editorial in the *Amherst Daily News* of April 14, 1923: "The situation is a rather serious one. The change is effective Sunday at 2 a.m. but not a word as yet. If lives are lost, limbs broken, vehicles smashed, as a result of collisions, may not part of the blame be laid at the feet of those who failed to proclaim the change?"

The editorial continued on to criticize the Nova Scotia government for not advertising in newspapers a change in driving rules. A cynic might suggest that the newspaper had a vested interest in an increase in government advertising, as it would get most of that advertising.

The cynic would be ignoring the seriousness of the situation. Only one day later, at exactly 2:00 a.m. on Sunday April 15, 1923, all traffic in Nova Scotia was to move from the left-hand side of the road to the right-hand side of the road.

The reason was the neighbouring province of New Brunswick. Much of Canada had adopted the right-hand-side driving rule. There were suggestions that Nova Scotia's failure to follow suit was hurting tourism because other Canadians were afraid they'd get in accidents. New Brunswick changed to right-hand-side traffic in December 1922 and since then, drivers crossing the border between the two provinces had to remember to switch over. It was confusing and, at times, dangerous.

Despite the editorial, Nova Scotia had in fact attempted to prepare drivers — automobiles were given "Keep to the Right" stickers for their windshields.

There were a few problems. Streetcar companies in eight Nova Scotia communities had to rebuild about one hundred streetcars to move the passenger doors from the left to the right-hand side. Tracks, switches, and drivers' controls also had to be altered in places. The Nova Scotia Tramways and Power Company Limited sued the province to recover the cost of changing the doors on all its streetcars.

As for the drivers, despite the hysteria whipped up by the newspapers, only a few minor accidents were reported. No lives were lost. No limbs were broken.

The oxen, however, had a hard go of it. The draft animals had been trained by their teamsters to walk on the left side of the road as they hauled their cargo. Not the brightest of beasts, oxen require years of training before they will obey commands. They could not be retrained to walk on the right. Something had to be done with them, so off they went to the slaughterhouse. In Lunenburg County, so the story goes, the extra supply of meat dropped prices so low that 1923 is remembered as the Year of Free Beef.

And the tunnel will become the subway system

Prospector, lumberjack, trapper, sailor, and dreamer Robert Allan Brown knew a good stake when he saw one. Looking for the next big find, the next good job, he worked and prospected his way from coast to coast in Canada around the turn of the century. In 1885, the forty-year-old Brown was prospecting about twelve kilometres north of Grand Forks in British Columbia when he spotted a red-capped mountain. That could mean one thing — iron ore. And perhaps also gold, silver, and copper.

Brown wasn't one to do things by halves. He staked claims all over the mountaintop and named his holdings Volcanic City. One-half of Volcanic City, he figured, would be needed for the hundreds of smelters treating the riches of ore inside the mountain. It would take six railways to move the ore out. With all the money he made, he would eliminate poverty in Canada, Brown promised. All he needed to do first was dig a long tunnel into the side of the mountain.

Brown's claim attracted the attention of investors from the U.S. The Olive Mining and Smelting Company gathered $20 million in capital to bond Brown's property. An 1895 Department of Mines report promised that "work on a very extensive scale is shortly expected."

Two years later, that extensive scale of work amounted to a 345-foot tunnel that had yet to hit the ore.

By 750 feet, however, some ore was coming out and getting a fairly good seven dollars of ore to the ton. That brought other investors and

Worst name ever

If Canadian history teaches us anything, it's this — don't tempt fate.

Case in point: naming your town Happy Valley.

The idea behind the town seemed sound. Some workers at Falconbridge Nickel wanted to escape life in the company town, Falconbridge, which is just northeast of Sudbury, Ontario.

The independent workers built a community in a valley just south of the company town, but they couldn't escape the company.

Sulphur fumes from the smelter often sank into the valley. During temperature inversions, when warm air forces cool air to the ground, the fumes got worse. It didn't help that the valley walls kept the air from moving.

By the seventies, pollution was turning Happy Valley into Death Valley. There were once so many trees the area was also known as Spruce Valley. But the trees were dying. People were worried pollution was killing them too. The town took the plant to court but lost.

Eventually, though, the province, the company, and the local government had to move the entire community to higher ground. There's nothing left of Happy Valley but abandoned houses and one bitterly ironic name.

other mining companies. By 1904, the tunnel was 800 feet long, yet the true vein had yet to be struck.

That was about as far as the tunnel went.

Brown never did find the rich vein of ore promised by the red cap. And his city never sprang up on the side of the mountain, either. The only thing Volcanic Mountain gave birth to was a $65,000 lawsuit Brown waged against people who said the claim was worthless.

Brown continued wandering and prospecting. He hit it rich several times but always seemed to end up back in the wilderness, prospecting. He died in the bush in 1931 at the age of eighty-six.

Oops, wrong mountain

"Being well rested by one o'clock, I set out with the view of ascending what seemed to be the highest peak on the north," wrote botanist David Douglas during his crossing of Athabasca Pass in 1827.

"Its height does not seem to be less than 16,000 or 17,000 feet [5,000 metres] above the level of the sea."

On top, about seven hours after he started climbing, he noted, "The view from the summit is of too awful a cast to afford pleasure. Nothing can be seen, in every direction as far as the eye can reach, except mountains towering above each other, rugged beyond description. This peak, the highest yet known in the northern continent of America, I feel a sincere pleasure in naming 'Mount Brown,' in honour of R. Brown, Esq., the illustrious botanist."

Douglas noticed a mountain to the south, almost as high.

"This I named Mount Hooker…"

So went Douglas's record of discovery of the highest points in Canada, indeed in all of North America. Or so everyone thought for the next seventy years.

Apparently, Douglas had based his estimates of the heights of the mountains on those of an earlier traveller who had lost his barometer.

Douglas didn't have the best eyesight, but he would have been hard pressed not to have noticed that other mountains in vicinity were obviously taller than those he named Brown and Hooker.

When Douglas's book and associated maps recounting his experiences in Canada's mountains were published, Mount Brown and Mount Hooker became well known.

The two mountains became alpine seductresses, always calling but hard to visit.

"A high mountain is always a seduction but a mountain with a mystery is doubly so … I studied the atlas and saw Mounts Brown and Hooker … [and] I longed to visit them," wrote Toronto geology professor Arthur Coleman.

In 1893, during his third summer of explorations, Coleman finally reached the pass where the mountains were supposed to rise, but the highest mountain he could find nearby was only about 2,800 metres high.

"What had gone wrong with these two mighty peaks that they should shrink seven thousand feet in altitude and how could anyone, even a botanist like Douglas, make so monumental a blunder?" mused Coleman.

The mystery of the highest peaks endured. J. Monroe Thorington, a mountaineer who first came to the Rockies in 1924, wrote, "When I was little, when you were a school-child, geography books taught that the highest mountains of North America — Mount Brown and Mount Hooker — lifted their unsurpassed heights on either side of Athabasca Pass."

This mythical pair had been talked about for so long and appeared on so many maps that the legend did not die easily. Even experienced Rockies mountaineers such as Walter Wilcox and Norman Collie still believed they may have existed and continued the search.

Finally fed up, Collie searched the libraries of England for Douglas's original account. He noticed that Douglas claimed to have climbed Mount Brown in a single afternoon.

"If David Douglas climbed a 17,000 foot peak alone on a May afternoon," he wrote, "when the snow must have been pretty deep on the ground, all one can say is that he must have been an uncommonly active person," Collie wrote.

"For nearly seventy years they have been masquerading in every map as the highest peaks in the Canadian Rocky Mountains; they must now retire from that position, and Mts. Forbes, Columbia, Bryce, and Alberta will, in future, reign in their stead."

That put the wooden stake through the mountain monster myth that until then would not die.

Today, Mount Logan, of the Elias Mountains, in southern Yukon, is recognized as being the highest point in Canada. It's 5,954.8 metres tall.

Douglas is remembered as a fine botanist, so fine that the Douglas fir was named after him. He is not, however, remembered as a fine mountaineer.

SOURCES

BOOKS

Akrigg, G.P.V., and Helen Akrigg. *1001 British Columbia Place Names*. Vancouver: Discovery Press, 1973.

Baillie-Grohman, William A. *Fifteen years' sport and life in the hunting grounds of Western America and British Columbia*. London: H. Cox Publisher, 1900.

Blake, Bernard, ed. *Jane's Weapon Systems, 1987-88*. New York: McGraw-Hill, 1988.

Boyce, Gerald. *Eldorado: Ontario's First Gold Rush*. Toronto: Natural Heritage / Natural History Inc., 1992.

Brennan, Brian. *Boondoggles, Bonanzas and Other Alberta Stories*. Calgary: Fifth House Ltd., 2003.

Brown, Brian A. *Foresters: The Canadian Quest for Peace*. Erin, ON: Boston Mills Press, 1991.

Brown, J.J. *Ideas in Exile: A History of Canadian Invention*. Toronto: McClelland and Stewart, 1967.

Brown, Ron. *Ghost Towns of Ontario*. Langley, BC: Stagecoach Publishing, 1978.

Champlain, Samuel de. *Journals of Samuel de Champlain, Vol III*, 1615-1618. Edited by H.P. Biggar. Toronto: University of Toronto Press, 1971.

Coleman, Arthur Philemonm. *The Canadian Rockies: New and Old Trails*. Toronto: Henry Frowde, 1911.

Fortier, Margaret, and Allan Shute. *Riverdale: From Fraser Flats to Edmonton Oasis*. Edmonton: Tree Frog Press, n.d.

Fryer, Mary Beacock. *Battlefields of Canada*. Toronto: Dundurn Press, 1986.

Fryer, Mary Beacock. *More Battlefields of Canada*. Toronto: Dundurn Press, 1993.

Gibson, Dale, and Lee Gibson. *Substantial Justice: Law and Lawyers in Manitoba, 1670-1970*. Winnipeg. Peguis Publishers, 1972.

Graves, Donald E., ed. *Fighting for Canada: Seven Battles, 1758-1945*. Toronto: Robin Brass Studio, 2000.

Hoffer, Marilyn Mona, and William Hoffer. *Freefall: A True Story*. New York: St. Martin's Mass Market Paper, 1990.

Leggett, Robert. *Canals of Canada*. Vancouver: Douglas, David and Charles, 1976.

Long, Gary, and Randy Whiteman. *When Giants Fall: The Gilmour Quest for Algonquin Pine*. Huntsville, ON: Fox Meadow Creations, 1998.

Malcomson, Robert. *Lords of the Lake: The Naval War on Lake Ontario, 1812-1814*. Toronto: Robin Brass Studio, 1998.

Milke, Mark. *Tax Me, I'm Canadian: Your Money and How Politicians Spend It*. Calgary, AB: Thomas & Black, 2002.

O'Brien, Brendan. *Speedy Justice: The Tragic Last Voyage of His Majesty's Vessel Speedy*. Toronto: University of Toronto Press, 1992.

Ricks, David A. *Blunders in International Business*. Oxford, UK: Blackwell Business, 1999.

St. Laurent, Arthur. *Georgian Bay ship canal: report upon survey, with plans and estimates of cost, 1908*. Ottawa: C.H. Parmelee, 1909.

Thwaites, Rueben Gold, ed. *The Jesuit Relations and Allied Documents*. Vols. XXXIV and XXXV. New York: Pageant Book Company, 1959.

Young, Peter, "The Old Hastings Colonization Road," *The Country Connection*, Autumn 2004.

Yurkowski, Bruno. "Attitudes and Policies of Ontario Governments Towards Agricultural Colonization in the Clay Belt Districts, 1892-1940." Thesis, University of Western Ontario, 1972.

Webb, Michael. *Reginald Fessenden: Radio's Forgotten Voice*. Mississauga, ON: Copp Clark Pitman, 1991.

REPORTS

Bellamy, Madame Justice Denise. Final Report on the Toronto Computer Leasing Inquiry and the Toronto External Contracts Inquiry, September 12, 2005.

Deputy Minister's Report to Premier Calvert, Spudco, 2003.

Fraser Institute, Government Failure in Canada, 2005 report, a review of auditor general's reports, 1992-2005.

Report of Commissioner appointed to inquire into the Matter of the Second Narrows Bridge, Burrard Inlet, BC, 1930.

Report of the Auditor General of Canada, 1992 to 2005 inclusive.

Report of the Provincial Auditor of Saskatchewan, Spring 2000.

Report of the Auditor General of Prince Edward Island, Government's Involvement with Polar Foods International Inc., 2005.

Temiskaming and Northern Ontario Railway Commission, The Great Clay Belt of Northern Ontario, Toronto, circa 1912.

Temiskaming and Northern Ontario Railway Commission, A Plain tale of plain people, pioneer life in New Ontario, Toronto, circa 1913.

Toronto Island Airport Fixed Link Studies:
- 1965 Atkins Hatch Feasibility Study Toronto Islands Tunnel
- March 1977, Access Alternatives, Toronto Island Airport Study
- 1982 Joint Co-ordinating Committee, Toronto Island Airport Development, Toronto Island Airport Access Study
- Royal Commission on the Future of the Toronto Waterfront, 1989
- Toronto Island Airport Study, KPMG, 1991
- 1996 TC Centre Airport, Fixed Link Options and Issue
- 1997 Dillion Consulting Ltd, Final Evaluation of Alternatives for Fixed Link to the Toronto City Centre Airport
- 2002 Report to Waterfront Reference Group

ARTICLES

Burchill, John. "The Rat Portage War," Winnipeg Police Service, http://winnipeg.ca/police/history/story13.stm

Keith, John, "Blasted Dreams and Broken Hearts, the Hastings Colonization Road," *The Country Connection*, Summer 1992.

Keith, John. "Ruts and Mudholes: The Peterson Colonization Road," *The Country Connection*, Autumn 1992.

Keith, John, "Up the Addington Colonization Road," *The Country Connection*, Autumn 1993.

Keith, John, "Up the Blaze, the Opeongo Colonization Road," *The Country Connection*, Autumn 1991.

Macdonald, John, "Rediscovering the Bobcaygeon Road," *The Country Connection*, Autumn 1994.

McMicken, Gilbert. "The abortive Fenian raid on Manitoba: account by one who knew its secret history." Paper read before the Manitoba Historical Society, Winnipeg, MB, May 11, 1888.

Tache, Alexandre. An open letter from Archbishop Taché to the Hon. Gilbert McMicken. St. Boniface, MB: s.n., 1888?

WEBSITES

Lake Erie Shipwrecks: www.alcheminc.com/shipwrck.html
Encyclopedia Astronautica: www.astronautix.com/
CBC Archives: www.cbc.ca/archives
Manitoba Historical Society: www.mhs.mb.ca
PATSCAN (The Patent Experts): www.patscan.ca

NEWSPAPERS

Calgary Herald
Edmonton Journal
Edmonton Sun
Vancouver Province
Toronto Globe

COLOSSAL CANADIAN FAILURES

Toronto Globe and Mail
Midland Free Press
Collingwood Enterprise Bulletin
Barrie Examiner
Northern Advance
London Free Press
Windsor Star
Toronto Star
Detroit Free Press
Ottawa Citizen